The Best Journey in the World

Adventures in Canada's
High Arctic

Jim Lotz

Pottersfield Press, Lawrencetown Beach, Nova Scotia

Library and Archives Canada Cataloguing in Publication

Lotz, Jim, 1929-

The best journey in the world : adventures in Canada's high Arctic / Jim Lotz.

Includes bibliographical references.

ISBN 1-895900-76-X

1. Lotz, Jim, 1929-. 2. Ellesmere Island (Nunavut) – Description and travel.
3. Meteorologists – Canada – Biography. I. Title.

FC4345.E55Z49 2006   917.19'5   C2006-900155-3

Cover design: Gail LeBlanc

Cover photo: istockphoto

Pottersfield Press acknowledges the ongoing support of The Canada Council for the Arts, and the financial support of the Government of Canada through the Book Publishing Industry Development Program for our publishing activities. We also acknowledge the support of the Nova Scotia Department of Tourism, Culture and Heritage.

Pottersfield Press
83 Leslie Road
East Lawrencetown
Nova Scotia, Canada, B2Z 1P8
Website: www.pottersfieldpress.com
To order, phone 1-800-NIMBUS9 (1-800-646-2879)

Printed in Canada

This book is dedicated to the memory of
Brian Sagar
good friend and companion in Africa, the Arctic and
places in between
and to the memory of:
Bob Christie
Jim Croal
Roger Deane
Fraser Grant
Trevor Harwood
Moreau "Max" Maxwell
Svenn Orvig
John Powell
Paul Walker.
It was a privilege to know them.

Acknowledgements

This book owes much to all my companions on Operation Hazen who shared their ideas and experiences with me, and especially to Dr. Geoffrey Hattersley-Smith, who was always just "Geoff" to us. I deeply appreciate the editorial assistance of Peggy Amirault and Julia Swan, who greatly improved the manuscript.

Photo credits: pp. 17, 125, 131, 139, 149, 150, 157, 208 – author; pp. 71, 73, 77, 78 – Department of National Defence; pp. 75, 121 – Royal Canadian Air Force; pp. 97, 111, 135, 176, 187, 191 – John Powell (Courtesy Margaret Powell); pp. 146, 181 – Geoff Hattersley-Smith; pp. 108, 114 – Courtesy Dick Harington. Every effort has been made to identify the copyright holders of the photographs. The author would appreciate any information and corrections.

The map on p. 38 is from "Northern Ellesmere Island: A Study in the History of Geographical Discovery" by Jim Lotz in *The Canadian Geographer* VI(3-4), 1962. The map on p. 182 is from "Operation Hazen: The First Summer, and the Winter Party" by Jim Lotz in *Canadian Geographical Journal* Vol. LXIII No. 2, (pp. 40-51), August 1961. The map on p. 184 is from "Operation Hazen – The Second Summer" by Jim Lotz in *Canadian Geographical Journal* Vol. LXIII No. 3 (pp. 101-111).

Contents

Prologue

In "the land beyond the land of the people"

The beauty and serenity hit you as soon as you get off the plane and it leaves you in awe . . . The Arctic provides the perfect opportunity for a person to know himself, his God and his creation.

— Josef Svoboda, *Ecology of a Polar Oasis*

At midnight on April 28, 1957, I jumped out of the rear doors of a Royal Canadian Air Force "Flying Boxcar" into twenty-five centimetres of crystalline snow on the surface of Lake Hazen in northern Ellesmere Island. Here, at 81° 49' N, the snow sparkled like a million diamonds under the midnight sun. The temperature hovered around -40°C.

The Inuit call northern Ellesmere Island "the land beyond the land of the people." Even the ancestors of these hardy people found life here too difficult and left when the climate cooled about four hundred years ago. After the plane departed, I looked around and saw nothing but white on white on white. The snow-covered lake surface merged with a low plateau to the east and hills to the west. Beyond these hills rose white mountains from which glaciers oozed towards the lake. I had travelled back in space and time to a primeval wilderness, to the morning of the world, to the ice age. Utter silence prevailed, and I wondered how I would survive in this harsh and empty land. I looked down. There, imprinted in the snow, were the marks of the paws and tail of some small animal, probably a lemming. If this creature could survive in this hostile environment, then so could I. Searching the clear blue sky, I saw another Flying Boxcar, its silver skin twinkling in the sun. It landed and disgorged tents, food boxes and equipment.

And so Operation Hazen, part of Canada's contribution to the International Geophysical Year of 1957-58, began. A few travellers had preceded us, including Lieutenant Adolphus Washington Greely, leader of the ill-fated 1881 Lady Franklin Bay Expedition. We entered a remote, unknown part of Canada that appeared locked in eternal ice and snow when we arrived, but turned into a bountiful land with rich vegetation during the brief, warm summer. While we could draw upon the findings of the Greely Expedition and the observations of the few other travellers who had passed through this land, the Lake Hazen basin and the nearby glacier and ice cap offered a pristine environment for research.

The lake sat in the middle of an Arctic oasis, which resembled Shangri-la during the summer. Here birds, plants and flowers could be studied in a place where humans had seldom intruded. Expedition members would establish baselines for such things as the status of the glaciers and the number of muskoxen that roamed in this land at the very edge of Canada. We had one foot in the heroic age of polar exploration and the other in the modern scientific era. We lived as once the Inuit did, in cramped, uncomfortable tents, ignored clock time, drove dogs and sang and talked away the evenings. The first residents of this part of Ellesmere Island scoured the land for anything that would ensure their survival. Our quest focused on acquiring new knowledge, new experiences, new insights into nature.

We did not seek adventure, the usual reason given by those who go to extreme places. Adventure sometimes found us, and we had some hairy moments

The concept of the International Geophysical Year originated with Lieutenant Karl Weyprecht of the Austro-Hungarian Navy. As co-leader of that empire's North Pole Expedition of 1872-74, he had wintered on the ice of the Barents Sea. Weyprecht concluded that polar research had to change direction. Instead of nations striving to plant their flags at higher and higher latitudes, they should engage in coordinated programs of scientific research using standardized observations.

Weyprecht's suggestion resulted in the First International Polar Year of 1882-83. The Americans sent expeditions to Point Barrow, Alaska, and Lady Franklin Bay in northern Ellesmere Island. German scientists studied Baffin Island, Austrian ones Jan Mayen Island. The Swedes, Russians, Dutch, Danes, Norwegians, Finns, British, and French also participated in the first IPY. In addition to scientific research, some of the expeditions carried out old-fashioned exploration, adding details of unknown lands to the map. The Lady Franklin Bay venture, which explored northern Ellesmere Island and northern Greenland, was the only expedition that lost members; only six men survived of the twenty-five who spent three years in the High Arctic.

During the Second International Polar Year of 1932-33, forty-four nations participated in a coordinated scheme of research. Frank Davies spent a year carrying out geophysical observations at Chesterfield Inlet in the then Northwest Territories during the Second IPY. He had also served with Byrd in the Antarctic. As the director of the Defence Research Board, he was one of the prime movers of Operation Hazen. The IPY became the IGY – International Geophysical Year – when its scope expanded to cover equatorial regions.

We received our official orders, dated April 16, 1957, a few days before we left Ottawa for the High Arctic. They listed the nine members of the 1957 party and stated: "The operation is planned as part of the Canadian IGY programme and for the purpose of certain military studies in the area."

The military studies involved identifying landing sites for planes and took up very little time. Operation Hazen, a pure science, curiosity-driven venture, concentrated on finding new knowledge about northern Ellesmere Island. It was rationalized as a way of exerting Canada's control over the High Arctic.

The Defence Research Board, a branch of the Department of National Defence, sponsored Operation Hazen, and drew specialists from universities and government departments. Sergeant Dave Engel of the Army's Royal Canadian Engineers went with the first party to put in a landing strip on Lake Hazen. Roger Deane of the University of Toronto, a limnologist, would study the lake and Bob Christie from the Geological Survey of Canada would carry out a reconnaissance of the island. The four other members of the 1957 party – Geoff Hattersley-Smith, the leader; Fraser Grant of the University of Toronto, the geophysicist; Keith Arnold, a surveyor from the Topographical Survey; and myself as glacial meteorologist (a jumped-up weather observer) – would spend the summer on the Gilman Glacier. We would be joined later by Hal Sandstrom and John Filo, two geophysics students from the University of Toronto.

A party of four would winter at the base camp on Lake Hazen. If all went well, a larger expedition would be mounted in the summer of 1958. Things did go well and I returned to Ellesmere Island in that year. In 1959, I spent the summer on the ice shelf attached to its north coast as glacial meteorologist with the Canada-US Ellesmere Island Ice Shelf Expedition, a miserable experience; I lived for four months in a trailer several kilometres north of Ward Hunt Island. In 1960, I returned to the Gilman Glacier with Geoff and spent three weeks there and travelling around the central ice cap.

Glaciers act like giant thermometers. If they are increasing in size and thickness, this signals a cooling of the climate. If they shrink, the climate must be warming up. There is a vast amount of panic these days about climate change and the warming of the Arctic. The Ward Hunt Ice Shelf began to break up in 1961-62, and the process accelerated over the next forty years. Polar bears are having problems finding seals as the amount of ice in the Arctic shrinks. That's good news if you are a seal. There are other costs and benefits to global warming in the Canadian North. Permafrost is melting under northern settlements and trees, insects and other creatures are moving north. From cores extracted from glaciers, you can see evidence of past periods of warming and cooling of the earth's climate. Some scientists claim that climatic change is normal. The burning of fossil fuels may play a small or a large part in global warming – as might the methane expelled by animals such as cows. A scientist in Environment Canada who has been monitoring climatic change for twenty years concluded: "This is like doing a 20,000-piece [jigsaw] puzzle. Every day new pieces come in but you have to put them in the context of all the other pieces." Our work on Operation Hazen provided a few of these pieces.

In contrast to the Canadian venture, the American ice shelf expedition in 1959 was directed at gaining practical results, although its goal was concealed with mention, in our orders, of carrying out geophysical research. If the Cold War turned hot, the Americans planned to send bombers over the pole to attack targets in the Soviet Union and might need landing sites for returning planes. The ice shelf expedition provided a classic example of the military planning the next war on the basis of what happened in the last one. During the 1960s, the missile threat replaced that posed by bombers. Later the ice shelf started to break up and bits of it floated into the Arctic Ocean. Nothing of practical value emerged from this American expedition – and very little of scientific value.

This book tells the story of Operation Hazen and something about the ice shelf expedition. It makes mention of other polar ventures in comparing what happened on them to our experiences in northern Ellesmere Island. I trace the path that led me from working-class Liverpool, England, to West Africa and on to Canada. I've always longed to know what lay around the next corner and at various times have held twenty-five different jobs. Chapters 1 and 2 disclose how and why I joined Operation Hazen, and outline the geography of northern Ellesmere Island and the history of its exploration. Our journey to Lake Hazen and the move to the Gilman Glacier forms part of Chapter 3.

The next two chapters tell of my companions, human and canine. In them, I ruminate on why men, and increasingly women, go to the Arctic. "Life on the Ice" outlines how a scientific expedition operates, although things have changed greatly in recent years and life in the polar region is much more comfortable. The cold, white land into which we intruded in the spring changed radically as the summer warmth flooded this Arctic oasis.

The chapter on "Discoveries and Mysteries" relates what we found during our stay in northern Ellesmere Island. Our research only touched the surface of this part of Canada. We established some base lines for future studies, preparing the way for those who would follow us. We encountered many mysteries that we could not explain.

The last chapter describes leaving the glacier and the base camp. Winter came to the higher reaches of the land as we prepared to leave in August. The short summer brought forth new life, and soon the landscape would return to what it looked like when first we arrived – pure, white, inaccessible, one of the harshest and loveliest places on earth. On May 24, 1999, my wife Pat and I attended a reunion of some of the members of the expedition. An epilogue covers what happened to them and other participants and to me after 1958.

Time in the polar regions marks you for life. You never forget its silences, its awesomeness, the feeling of having tested yourself to the limits and emerged stronger from the ordeals and dangers you endured. Apsley Cherry-Garrard, a member of Scott's last expedition to Antarctica in 1910-12, wrote *The Worst Journey in the World*, a classic of polar exploration. With "Birdie" Bowers and Edward Wilson – who died with Robert Scott on the return from the South Pole, eleven miles from One Ton Depot – Cherry-Garrard went in search of penguin eggs in the middle of the Antarctic winter. They suffered incredible hardships – his teeth cracked, the tent blew away in a blizzard and the party nearly perished. The three men recovered the embryos of emperor penguins to verify a crackpot theory that the creatures formed the missing link between reptiles and birds. When Cherry-Garrard took the eggs to a London museum, no one expressed interest in them. He wrote of Scott's expedition: "The first year . . . was not the one long idyll that later accounts suggest. Few expeditions ever are. The records are sanitized as a matter of course."

My account of Operation Hazen has not been sanitized. Cherry-Garrard accurately reflected my feelings about work in the polar regions when he described it as "the physical expression of an intellectual passion . . . a great unrest."

These days, adventure tourists land at Tanquary Fiord, and walk along the Musk Ox Way to the Lake Hazen basin. They literally follow in the footsteps of the Inuit who passed this way over four thousand years ago. Like me, these travellers experience the best journey in the world, one that takes you to the limits of the earth and of your own being. Here you come to understand the mysteries of the land, of yourself and of your companions. And you recognize the necessity to keep on exploring them in an ongoing quest for tranquility and the opportunity to live in harmony with all other humans and all of creation.

Chapter 1

Occupation – Explorer

Something hidden, go and find it
Something lost behind the Ranges
Lost and waiting for you. Go!

Rudyard Kipling, "The Explorer"

How did I become a member of an Arctic expedition? Growing up in working class Britain, I'd read about the exploits of Robert Scott and Ernest Shackleton and been inspired by them. In his introduction to *British Adventure*, Nigel Tangye claims: "Our attitude to adventure is a puzzle to men of other lands. To them it is frequently illogical. To us, too, if we think about it, it is also illogical. But we admire the spirit of a man who attempts the impossible, and whether he has as much stupidity as spirit does not really matter." Noting that Scott's expedition was marred by poor leadership, bad planning and inefficient operation, Tangye adds: "Scott's failure to reach the South Pole before [Roald] Amundsen, and the loss of his party, fills a place in our hearts much bigger than if he had been successful." In recent years, Ernest Shackleton has been the subject of TV programs and movies. He lost his ship, *Endurance*, in the Antarctic ice but brought all his men home safely. Otherwise his expedition was a failure – the party never set foot on Antarctica.

British polar expeditions recruited upper class twits, Oxbridge graduates, naval officers and ratings, grizzled seamen and rich and well-connected amateurs. They set out for unknown lands in search of adventure. Even if they failed to reach their goals, they returned to fame and fortune: many British officers who served on polar expeditions rose to the rank of admiral.

How could I ever join the ranks of such distinguished adventurers? And yet I did become an explorer – officially. Election enumerators visited my apartment building in Montreal in 1957 while I was absent. The superintendent gave them my occupation as "Explorer."

My British upbringing imbued me with ideas about adventure and journeys to distant places. The path that led me from Liverpool, England, to northern Ellesmere Island zigged and zagged; it was never linear. From my parents I derived certain values and from my experiences in England, Africa and elsewhere I gained ideas and insights that proved useful in the Arctic.

My father had a strong sense of discipline, duty and comradeship. He served with the Liverpool Scottish during the First World War. His battalion went over the top at Hooge on the Western Front on June 16, 1915, losing four hundred of its men and twenty officers. Dad seldom spoke of his time at war. He told me that an officer, standing next to him, was shot through the head. Slightly wounded, my father returned to England as a musketry instructor. He taught recruits how to shoot and then joined the King's African Rifles in 1917 and spent the rest of the war chasing German

Jim Lotz, back home in Liverpool after hitchhiking across North Africa in 1950.

soldiers in East Africa. He caught malaria, which stayed with him for the rest of his life.

At the end of the war, Dad returned to England and found a steady job as an attendant in the left-luggage office at a Liverpool railway station. He kept this job until he retired, working three shifts round the clock with one Sunday off every three weeks. He hated the job, but cycled through the blitzes during the Second World War to relieve his mates so they could return to their families. Many nights, coming off shift, he went out firefighting as incendiary bombs fell on our neighbourhood.

My mother came from Oldmeldrum, a small village in Aberdeenshire, Scotland. Her father had been a cottar, a farm servant, who developed entreprenurial instincts, became known as "The Potato King of Oldmeldrum" and acquired a small grocery story. Mum came from a family of ten, the only one of six sisters who married. The Scots have always valued education and I received every encouragement to pursue mine. While I was growing up, the idea of going to university was as remote as the possibility of going on an Arctic expedition. My brother left school at fourteen and took an office job. I wanted something different, something that did not involve sitting on my backside all day and waiting for retirement. My father loathed his job and I saw how he, a highly intelligent man, simply did what he had to do to sustain his family and took his small pleasures when he could. He was forty-three when I was born and always somewhat remote; during some weeks, because of his shift, my brother and I seldom saw him.

The family split up when World War II broke out in 1939. My brother went with his school to Holyhead in Wales and I was evacuated to my mother's village. I soon became an outsider with no friends of my own age. The local youths mocked my name ("shallots") and my Liverpool accent. If the teacher left the class and it descended into chaos, the headmaster dashed down the hall. The only voice he could identify in the clamour was mine so I was strapped on the hand many times. I soon developed an Aberdeenshire brogue, but by that time had become a solitary youngster who took long walks into the countryside.

The love of my five aunts offset my isolation – was I the child they never had? – and the healthy life and good food turned me from a somewhat scrawny child into a strong and plump one. In 1940, I returned to Liverpool to take high school exams and for the next few years spent my winters there and my summers in Oldmeldrum. One day I jumped on a lorry and became an assistant to the driver. Hauling bags of grain and coal around built up my physique.

I hated my home town and loved Scotland. At one time I thought about becoming a forester, spending days in a fire tower, surveying my domain, with plenty of time to read. My life alternated between a grimy port city and rural Scotland. In May 1941, a bomb just missed our house, destroying the three next door, killing six people. We never knew their names. They were buried with hundreds of other anonymous dead in a mass grave. In contrast to the impersonality of urban life, everyone in Oldmeldrum knew everyone else's business.

One thing became certain as I grew up. I would get the hell out of Liverpool as soon as possible. From the ferry landings at the Mersey River I could see its estuary. Beyond lay the world and I wanted to go there, to visit distant lands and exotic places about which I read in *Wide-World* magazine. I developed a particular interest in polar exploration, feeling drawn to those cold and harsh ends of the world.

I left home in March 1947, at the request of His Majesty, conscripted into the Royal Air Force for two years. After basic training, which I thoroughly enjoyed, I was assigned to the trade of radio fitter. As my brother correctly observed, "You couldn't fit a sneck (latch) on a duck's arse." I had taken history and geography in my last two years of school, had no technical training and no interest in radio. After forty weeks' training, I had only the vaguest notion what it involved. Recalling the words of George Bernard Shaw – "Those who can, do, those who can't, teach" – I applied to be an instructor. I did well in the exam and remained at No. 1 Radio School, Cranwell, for the rest of my time in the services.

After being demobilized in 1949, I spent two months hitchhiking around France before entering the honours geography program at Manchester University in the fall. I have a terrible sense of direction, so the choice of geography seemed to me a natural one and fitted into my desire to travel the world. In the summer of 1950 I decided to visit Iceland. I read the wrong information on the ferry service, believed it would break my budget, so hitchhiked through Morocco and Algeria instead. Graduating in 1952, I had no idea what to do with my geography degree. Most of my fellow graduates became teachers. I wanted adventure.

A call came from the United Africa Company (UAC), a Unilever subsidiary, seeking graduates as managers for their trading posts in West Africa. This offered a chance for adventure and travel – and for serving others. World War II turned many members of my generation into idealists. We saw the triumph of democracy over totalitarianism and the emergence of new technology such as atomic power that we believed would be used in the cause of international peace and fellowship. The Labour government struggled to bring this new world into being by expanding the role of the state but utopia did not arrive and life after the war became incredibly grey and dreary. I believed that by becoming a trader in Africa I could help people there by giving them a fair price for what they produced and selling them what they needed at reasonable rates. I impressed the company recruiters with my knowledge of West Africa, derived entirely from books: I knew people in the northern regions needed white cloth and lots of salt.

I was hired and told to wait to be called to London for training. While doing so I spent two weeks on the RAF Reserve near Dunbar. The equipment I was assigned to was not working when I arrived at the station. And it was not working when I left. I went grouse beating in the Highlands of Scotland for a month and learned a useful lesson from one of these birds. We tramped across the soggy ground, shouting and beating the heather, driving the grouse to the butts. Here stood members of the local aristocracy who shot them down. On one beat, I heard a rustle in the heather. A grouse took off – away from the butts. It survived by not panicking and going in the opposite direction to its doomed companions.

After a vigorous spell on the Scottish moors, usually in pouring rain, I spent three restful weeks in London, learning how to be a manager. I flew to Lagos, Nigeria, and was driven three hundred and twenty-five kilometres north to Oshogbo to serve as assistant to the manager of UAC's post there. Among other things, I learned how to check cocoa beans to determine if they were ready to be harvested. I liked the Africans with whom I came in contact, but soon realized that I was a manager not because of competence but because I was white. I had barely settled into my bungalow when the UAC manager decided he did not need me. This disagreeable individual, a Canadian, showed me no friendship and I was happy to leave the wet tropical climate for the drier one of northern Nigeria.

In Kano, I joined UAC's service department, a catch-all agency. I checked large pyramids of peanuts awaiting shipment to ports, visiting them at night and pumping up the Tilley lamps that were supposed to deter thieves, and waking up the guards. I supervised the weighing of pigs at a company farm. Since Islam forbids its followers to eat pork, how UAC ended up rearing these animals in a mainly Moslem area never became clear to me. I greeted and briefed visitors at the airport, and saw them settled in their quarters.

After a few months in Kano, I went north to Katsina to supervise a string of small, African-run trading posts owned by the company. Here, at the edge of the desert, I moved into a land of endless horizons, of infinite space and emptiness. Baobab trees thrust their trunks out of the bare earth like dead hands reaching for the sky in a Daliesque landscape. This land spoke to something deep in my psyche, some unknown, uncharted dimension whose limits I strove continually to explore.

I learned a lesson in economics here. Our store manager at Katsina would place a lantern on a scale. Out of the night came donkeys laden with peanuts grown in the French colony to the north of us (now Niger). The French authorities did not like this practice. They insisted that our customers send their crops to Dakar in Senegal, more than two thousand kilometres to the west. For a while we stopped buying French peanuts. Then someone filled a customs officer with arrows and the donkeys again began to come in the night.

I enjoyed my work with UAC, got on well with the Africans and became a member of a group of young bachelors making their way in the West African trade; however, I became increasingly aware of how the company, which dominated merchandising and produce-buying activities in the region, exploited its customers. One day in Sokoto I received a message from Kano to raise the price of gasoline by a few pennies. We had monopoly control of that product, so I visited every store we supplied on "the beach" – the strip where they were located – and told the owners they had to raise their price for gasoline. Our post sold salt, cloth, hardware, perfume, pomades and other goods. We totalled up their delivered cost then added the Merchandise Expense Reserve, a euphemism for profit.

Just as an army needs able sergeants for its efficient operation, so UAC relied on a number of highly competent chief clerks. Many of them carried white managers who could not run a market stall efficiently, let alone a trading post. The company provided housing for expatriate managers. In theory, UAC sought to "Africanize" its management staff. An African clerk, promoted to manager, found his new home invaded by relatives who came to stay, making him poorer than before. The company could have given African managers a housing allowance. This would have had them earning more than their white counterparts, so was totally unacceptable.

With its near-monopoly of trade, UAC had become complacent. Why bother to be efficient when profits rolled in year after year? Why train your staff when Africans begged for clerical jobs? Why improve your products and your merchandising efforts when you controlled so much of the market?

I saw many expatriates play the colonial game, acting in lordly ways, despising Africans who struggled to retain their dignity. The Africans I met wanted to be respected and I liked many of them. Some managers and colonial officials ignored the feelings of the people they worked with, dominating Africans and expecting them to do their bidding. As Marshall McLuhan put it: "You become what you behold." How long would it be before I started behaving like these other colonials? After ten years with UAC, you could leave with their portion of the pension contributions as well as your own. I saw many managers, especially married ones, simply hanging on, going through the motions, waiting for that blessed day when they could return to England, home and beauty, after their exile in the colonies.

Under the placid surface of the country lay a vast discontent with colonial rule. An African told me, "We would rather be badly ruled by our own people than well ruled by you British."

According to the old axiom, "You can postpone your moment of truth – but you can't avoid it." My moment came during the Kano riots in May 1953. They came as a complete surprise to the company and the colonial government, which were unprepared to deal with them. All whites, sworn in as special constables, received helmets and batons and were told to stop the widespread looting. The riots stemmed from a clash between southern Nigerians, who demanded independence from Britain in 1955, and northern Nigerians, the Hausa, who had no deadline in mind and were quite happy under the system of indirect rule put in place by the British. Through it, traditional rulers still exercised a great deal of power at the local level. A southern politician came to Kano and whipped ethnic fears and hatred.

At first, the riots had almost a festive air. I came across a mob emptying a row of shops, picked up a branch of a tree, threw it at the looters – and missed. They all gave me a rousing cheer for my efforts and went back to stealing anything they could lay their hands on. Soon, the killing began. Northerners hunted southerners who lived in their areas and took them apart with machetes. Southerners dragged northerners from their homes, doused them with gasoline and set them on fire. We did what we could to stop the looting and the killing and that was far too little. I remember seeing a man attacked with machetes brought into a police post by six friends: any fewer and he would have fallen apart. Small traders who had little enough to sell lost everything.

With three other UAC managers, I drove past a Hausa mob outside the house of a southerner who had converted to Islam. We went to a nearby police post. Here sat two colonial officials with blank expressions on their faces. "There's a mob up the road, trying to kill someone," we told them. "Nothing we can do about that," one replied. They were afraid that the rioters would turn against any whites who tried to stop the killings. We went back to the besieged house, rescued the man and took him to hospital.

The general manager of Kano UAC called a meeting of managers and berated us for subduing the rioters. He felt that this did not constitute an effective form of customer relations. "What were we supposed to do?" I asked. "Ask them politely to desist from stealing and killing?" This question did not receive an answer. I'd come to Africa for adventure and I was certainly getting it! Before I left England, an old Africa hand gave me some good advice – "Keep your head cool and your stomach warm, your bowels open and your mouth shut." Three out of four wasn't bad.

The riots crystallized my discontent with UAC and colonial life. It was obvious that I was living in a dying social order where the company had its eye only on profit and the government did not worry if Africans killed each other. Another manager and I resigned. It soon became apparent that we had done something other managers wanted to do, so our act became a symbolic one. We could easily have withdrawn our resignation, but John Mackenzie Miller, a fiery Scot, and I were fed up with the attitude of the company and realized that there was no way back for us.

Returning to England, I found employment opportunities for geographers very scarce and took a job in a factory. When my boss discovered I had a university degree, he fired me. The Fifties, a grim, dismal decade in Britain, spawned "angry young men." The class-ridden society and economy failed to adapt to change as the Germans and Japanese rebuilt their factories with the most modern equipment. The Labour government nationalized the railways and the coal mines that had been driven into the ground by their owners. Then the government confronted a problem. They wanted the workers to take over the nationalized industries and become managers. But workers did not want to become bosses. Whatever money they made would be offset by social costs when they could no longer mingle as equals with their mates.

I applied for a job as trainee manager with British Railways, only to be told that the positions were restricted to former officers. As everyone knew, they were "good with men." I spent months in limbo, sending out numerous handwritten applications for jobs that received no reply. Before Christmas 1953, I took a job selling toy trains in a large department store – quite a comedown from my last position as merchandising manager of a trading post.

I vowed that if I did not get a job six months after leaving Africa, I would go to Canada as what is now known as an economic refugee. I had only the vaguest notions about the country – Mounties, Eskimos, wheat, lumber, the Rockies, the Arctic, cold weather. A Canadian immigration official assured me that it was "a great big country growing up all over." I had a quick medical examination and was on my way in late March 1954, aboard the *Queen Mary*. I planned, like many immigrants, to land in New York and make my way to Toronto. A dock strike in New York diverted the liner to Halifax, Nova Scotia, where I landed at Pier 21. I decided to go to Ottawa and offer my services to the federal government.

As the immigrant train headed west, I saw railway workers driving to stations in their cars. My father spent his life working on the railways and never had more than a bicycle. My first impression of my new country was that there was an awful lot of it and most of it was covered in forest.

I arrived in Ottawa on April 1, 1954, rented a room and went in search of work, and soon discovered that I had to be in Canada for five years before being eligible to work for the federal government. At the Defence Research Board, Trevor Harwood, head of its Arctic Section, gave me some good advice: "Go back to university. You'll get nowhere in Canada until you have a Canadian degree." Harwood later became the main organizer of Operation Hazen and I came to know him well.

Finally, with my money running out, I found a job with Canadian Aero Services, assembling aerial photographs into large mosaics. That lasted three months before I was fired for falling asleep while being instructed on how to use a new piece of equipment. A fellow English immigrant and co-worker claimed you had to have a car to be a true Canadian, so I had bought what turned out to be a lemon, a Morris Oxford with a defective starter. Driving back to my boarding house after being fired, I edged carefully into an intersection. With only a provisional driving license, I should have had a qualified driver with me. Out of the corner of my eye, I saw another car heading towards me. It hit me – or I hit it.

The details of the collision are a trifle vague in my mind. The Morris spun one hundred and eighty degrees and tried to climb a stop sign. Somewhere in its twisting course, my hip hit the door handle and I flew out of the vehicle. At the time, I was doing a lot of judo and rolled as I hit the ground. My friend – who had also been fired – was following me and saw the accident. Aghast, he thought I was a goner. Then, through the dust, he caught a glimpse of me, on my hands and knees, searching for my glasses. Except for a bruise on my hip, I emerged unscathed. The lawyer of the driver who hit me – or who I hit – agreed to resolve the claim against me for a thousand dollars. I had saved very little, so I borrowed the money from my parents. Later I learned the federal government had funds to assist newcomers with financial problems. The bureaucrat who told me about it added, "Of course, we don't tell anyone about it."

Jobless and in debt, I set about finding employment. Replying to a newspaper ad, I applied for the position of advertising manager with IGA, the food wholesaler, seduced by visions of life in this glamorous occupation. I had a most peculiar interview. "Is Manchester a good university?" asked the man who became my boss. I assured him it was and got the job at $50 a week. Four days later, just as I settled into my office, the boss told me, "We've decided we don't need an advertising manager. But we have an opening for a billing clerk. You can have the job – at $40 a week." This may be what is known in the retail trade as "bait and switch."

Running out of money, I had no choice and agreed to take the lower-paying job. The company worked an eight-hour day, five days a week, but the boss added, "We stay late on Fridays to get out the newsletter and we come in on Saturday mornings. You don't have to do that, of course, but . . ." The message was plain. Each morning I set off for the company's offices in Alta Vista at seven in the morning. A long walk took me to Rideau Street where I boarded a bus. During the winter of 1954-55, the cold of Ottawa frostbit my ear, the only portion of my anatomy ever to be so affected. Leaving work at five, I seldom reached the boarding house before six in the evening.

The work proved agonizingly boring. The stores supplied by IGA sent in forms on which various items were listed, ticking off what they wanted. I went down the lists, noted these orders and totalled up the cost. Then I passed them to the senior clerk, Morris, a man I soon came to detest. He lorded over me, correcting my many mistakes without telling me how to do the job better. I found myself trapped and began to look for alternate employment.

But how could I go for an interview while I was working all the time? The car accident worked in my favour. My boss let me off one day to settle the damage claim. I applied for a job with the advertising office of Freimans, a large department store. My boss at IGA and the owner of the store discussed whether this new job – which paid $40 a week – was in my best interests. Was this concern for me – or paternalism?

On my first day, my new boss told me, "Grab a typewriter." This presented a problem: I did not know how to type. The woman I replaced had fewer skills than I did and I became a very fast two-finger typist. I soon decided I'd landed in another dead-end job with no hope of advancement. I met Harwood on the street one day. "Gone back to university yet?" he asked in typically brusque fashion. When I admitted I had not he said, "Humph" and walked away. A lucky chance helped me to follow Harwood's advice. The other copywriter did not want to work on Saturdays. I covered that day, and took off another during the week.

I wrote to the University of Toronto and McGill University, asking about the possibilities of stipends for graduate work. Dr. Ken Hare, chair of McGill's geography department, invited me to Montreal for an interview. In the 1950s, few Canadians wanted to work in the north. We sing in our national anthem about "the true north strong and free" and see that region as part of our identity. But most of us live within one hundred and fifty kilometres of the

American border and view the north as a cold and barren wilderness – or a place to go and "clean up and clear out."

McGill had a Subarctic Research Laboratory at Schefferville, an iron-mining town in Quebec's Ungava Pensinsula near the Labrador border. Hare, a highly entrepreneurial academic, persuaded the Department of Transport, which ran weather stations, to hire graduate students to take meteorological observations there. If I spent the summer of 1955 at the laboratory as a weather observer, I'd earn enough money to pay my university fees and have a little bit left over. During the school term, I'd have a job at the observatory on the McGill campus at $125 a month and work towards my Master's degree in geography. I jumped at the offer.

All I knew about Ungava and the Labrador peninsula came from Robert Ballantyne's book of that name. I pictured myself wrestling bears, snowshoeing across barren lands, dragging canoes over portages and sitting around campfires in silent fellowship with fellow travellers and maybe an Indian or two. The reality of life at the McGill Subarctic Research Lab proved more mundane than this in some ways, more fascinating in others. The only dangerous experience I had came while canoeing with Jack Ives, the director, and his wife Pauline on John Lake. A sudden windstorm arose and waves threatened to swamp the craft. My two companions, skilled canoeists, knew exactly what to do: paddle furiously and keep the craft into the wind. I sat between them, serving as ballast.

During the summers of 1955 and 1956, in addition to doing weather observations, I became part of an interdisciplinary research team. We shared quarters and scientific findings on this wild, empty land while huge machines tore it apart and trains carried millions of tons of iron ore to Sept-Îles to be shipped to steel mills in the United States. Beyond the scars created by the mining machines lay a wilderness for us to explore and study. West of the town lay the Howells River. I crossed it with a companion and we took to the hills to avoid the mosquitoes and black flies. We found a cross on a high point. Had it been erected a hundred years ago by a missionary priest or set up to serve as a marker for a mineral survey?

The lab lay at the side of the airport, several kilometres from Schefferville. We seldom went there except for groceries. From the lab windows, we looked out on a seemingly limitless land where low ridges rolled to the horizon under grey sheets of scudding cloud. We had tapes of the symphonies of Sibelius, which I listened to while gazing out on the landscape, absorbed by the haunting sounds from a similar setting. In Ungava, nature ruled, as it had done for millions of years and humans, even with their most powerful machines, were mere transitory intruders. Sibelius' music captured this feeling of emptiness, harshness and infinite space. In 1967, I took part in Glenn Gould's CBC Radio program, *The Idea of North*. He ended it with the final crashing chords of Sibelius' *Fifth Symphony*, decisive echoes of this land we clung to by our fingertips.

Schefferville served as the main Ungava supply base for the Mid-Canada Line, built along the fifty-fifth parallel to give the United States a few minutes warning should Soviet bombers attack over the Arctic. At the weather station in the lab, we took observations of temperature, windspeed, cloud cover, barometric pressure, humidity and so on. We punched the data on to a tape and fed it into a teleprinter that banged away night and day. In Montreal, the decoded symbols formed the basis for synoptic weather charts. These came to the lab through the Mufax, an early form of fax machine, and were consulted by the resident meteorologist. He briefed the bush pilots who took supplies west and east to Mid-Canada Line stations. A very professional, easygoing, rather madcap bunch, they paid close attention to the weather, which could change within minutes.

I flew with one of them almost to the coast of Labrador in a Canso amphibian, also known as the PBY and the Catalina, robust planes that had served well in the Second World War. We landed on a lake and hastily discharged our cargo of timber. Then I stood behind the pilot as he revved the engines to full power. The Canso shook and shuddered as the engines roared. We began to move, faster and faster, bouncing on the water, spray splattering the windows. Then the plane rose gracefully and we headed for home. We saw below us small scratches in the endless forest where lay Mid-Canada sites, the only signs of human presence in this untracked land.

The north provides excellent conditions for studying the separate phenomenon and the interrelationships between them. In settled and temperate places, the land has been so altered by human presence that it's impossible to see connections between natural phenomena. In the taiga and the tundra, nature is laid bare and you can see the web of life and the interactions between all living things.

In the Subarctic, I learned that science involved endless instrument readings, a quest for patterns, a search to determine the shape and nature of the weather and the climate. Our observations went on twenty-four-hours a day, 365 days a year, for nature never takes a holiday. As the ice on Hudson Bay to the west broke up, rain-soaked clouds drifted across Ungava. The sky remained grey for days on end. Suddenly a high pressure system would build up and we'd have periods of CAVU – Ceiling and Visibility Unlimited. At night we sent up balloons with tiny lights attached to determine the height of the cloud layer. One keen observer tracked a light for an hour. He later learned that he had been, literally, following his star. On some nights the aurora borealis shimmered in the sky, great sheets of green, shifting as we watched a marvellous, mysterious display. Physicists with geophones sought to record the sounds generated by this celestial wonder.

Science advances as much from failures as from successes. There are no "breakthroughs" in research, only an endless search for patterns that can be replicated by others. For my Master of Science thesis, I studied soils and agriculture. Digging over a plot of land near the lab in 1956, I planted grains, grasses and vegetables. All died in midsummer. I walked the land, testing and mapping the thin taiga soils. The agricultural potential of the region was nil, but I wrote a small brochure on lawns and gardens in the Subarctic and distributed it to local residents.

This small initiative had an unexpected outcome. I sent a copy to Vilhjalmur Stefansson (1879-1962), then in residence at Dartmouth College in New Hampshire. Stef promoted the northward course of the British Empire and the "friendly Arctic" after leading three expeditions between 1906 and 1918. He travelled extensively in the Arctic, living off the land like the Inuit and believing that others could do the same. The explorer saw the Arctic Ocean as a polar Mediterranean. My small pamphlet supported his ideas of the fruitful north. He invited me to lecture at Dartmouth College on my work and treated me very hospitably.

A woman in the Yukon told me, "I'd go nuts if I did not have my flowers." It's the small, green touches and human things that matter in extreme environments, not great, abstract theories about northern development based on the idea of conquering nature or some such nonsense. You never conquer nature – you learn to live in and with it. In the North, you must cope with life in the Great

Outdoors and in the Little Indoors, the cramped quarters in which you live. Field work challenges your body. Living with others tests your spirit and soul. You confront nature at an elemental level in the North – and yourself and others as you live and work together. All polar narratives tell of the tensions that arise during expeditions. You experience selflessness and pettiness, great sacrifices and meanness in yourself and others.

At the Schefferville lab in 1955 we lived in cramped quarters, cooking in a small kitchen, sharing bedrooms where shift changes made sleep difficult. In the following year, the lab expanded and we had a living room where we could relax and shut out the perpetual chatter of the teletype. We also had a larger kitchen that made meal preparation, which we did ourselves, easier. Usually we got on well with each other, in part because of rotating shifts. Between eight-hour spells of weather observation, sleep and field work, we kept ourselves fully occupied.

Once in a while, tensions rose and we had problems. An observer, coming on shift, deliberately embarrassed the man from whom he took over by taking a reading of the cloud cover that contradicted the previous one. Estimating cloud height is a tricky business – you can do it by eye or use a simple piece of equipment. If someone made a mistake, you adjusted the next reading to cover it. We knew how important our observations were to pilots and did all we could to make them as accurate as possible. We sent in sheets with our monthly observations and received feedback from a central office. In time, we became very proficient weather observers and this experience stood me in good stead when I was recruited for Operation Hazen. I did not care for some of my colleagues, but unable to escape them, I made allowances for their peculiarities, just as they did for mine.

While I was on duty one day, another observer picked up a chair, intent on crowning the director. I removed it from his hands, saying "If you want to kill him, please do it outside where there's no risk of damaging the equipment." Back in Montreal, Ken Hare remarked that I had gained a reputation as a peacemaker and this may have been another reason for the invitation to join Operation Hazen.

While writing my thesis, I looked around for a job, with little success. A recruiter for Canadian National Railways looked over my résumé. It listed my many previous occupations – truck driver's assistant, mailman, farm labourer, trader, toy salesman, billing clerk, copywriter. I left out opera super, grouse beater and special constable. In 1957, such a diversity of jobs doomed anyone seeking steady employment. Today I would be considered to have the desirable qualities of adaptability, social, occupational and geographic mobility. Shaking his head, the man handed back my résumé, saying, "If we ever encounter any unusual tasks or challenges, we'll contact you."

I now had two degrees in geography and, at twenty-eight, still no idea what I was going to do with my life. Then the phone rang.

The call came from Dr. Svenn Orvig, a tall, affable Norwegian-born professor of meteorology and geography at McGill.

"Have you found a summer job – or a permanent one?" he asked.

"No," I replied.

"Do you want to go on an Arctic expedition?"

"Sure. What's involved?"

"Come up to my office and I'll tell you all about it."

Chapter 2

Going to Extremes

*I have heard it said that a well-managed expedition was noth-
ing but a glorified picnic with a spice of danger and our stay
[in Antarctica] has certainly upheld the truth of the remark.*
— Raymond Priestley,
geologist with Shackleton and Scott

I was recruited for Operation Hazen in typical British fashion —
someone asked me if I wanted to serve on it. In his office, Svenn
showed me a map of the Arctic and located Ellesmere Island on
it. I would be expected to set up a weather station on the Gilman
Glacier and take observations during the summer.

"Are you making me a definite offer?" I asked Svenn.

"Yes," he replied.

"Then I'm giving you a definite acceptance."

And so the course of my life for the next four years was set. We
did not discuss pay, equipment, the state of my health. My skills as

a weather observer and my willingness to go to the most northerly part of Canada sufficed for hiring me. My response to Svenn's offer echoed that of at least two other polar explorers. Raymond Priestley sat in the library of University College, Bristol, bored stiff. Nearby, a recruiter interviewed candidates for the position of geologist on Shackleton's 1907 *Nimrod* expedition. Finding no suitable individual, he asked Bart Priestley if his brother Raymond would be interested in going with Shackleton. The conversation that led Priestley to a distinguished academic career and a knighthood went as follows:

"How would you like to go to Antarctica?"

"I'd do anything to get out of this place."

Graham Rowley completed his fourth year at Cambridge University in 1935 and "had no idea what to do next." Tom Manning came to see him with a letter from the curator of the university's Museum of Archeology and Ethnology. It said: "This is to introduce Mr. Manning with whom, I hope, you will go to the Arctic. He will explain things to you." Rowley went north with Manning, charting unmapped lands in northern Baffin Island, travelling and living with the Inuit and making significant archeological discoveries; an island in Foxe Basin is named after him. He called the book about his time in the Arctic *Cold Comfort*.

I joined Operation Hazen because I did not have a job, and was flattered by the offer to go on an Arctic expedition – something I could never have dreamed about while growing up in England. My salary of three hundred dollars a month would go into my bank account and would carry me over the months after the expedition ended.

Map of northern Ellesmere Island: Geographical Features.

Canada's Hidden Dimension

Oh would you know how earth can be
A hell – go north of Eighty-three.
— Robert Service, "Death in the Arctic"

Svenn Orvig served as glacial meteorologist with expeditions to the ice caps of Baffin Island in 1950 and 1953, the first scientific ventures of this kind in the Canadian Arctic. Before this, with a few exceptions, most people had gone north to explore the land or claim it for Canada or race for the pole.

The Arctic Islands, "Canada's Hidden Dimension," – the title of a book of scientific papers edited by Dick Harington – lie north of 74°. They resemble a shattered arrowhead pointing towards northern Greenland. Only a handful of residents live there year-round at Resolute (pronounced "desolate" according to a sign we saw there), Eureka (a weather station), Grise Fiord (an Inuit settlement) and Alert (a military base and weather station). The Arctic Islands comprise one fifth of Canada's land mass; this harsh, barren region often does not appear on maps of the nation. Just under half of the area has no plants, birds or mammals. Ellesmere Island covers 196,236 square kilometres.

Northern Ellesmere Island lies beyond 80° N. At its tip, at 83° 06' 41" N lies Cape Columbia, the most northerly point of Canada. Robert E. Peary left from here on his 1908 journey to the North Pole. Modern pole vaulters use Ward Hunt Island as a base because it's easier to land a plane near it than at Cape Columbia; the island where we built a hut in 1959 now resembles the base of Mount Everest, with piles of discarded junk left lying around by travellers.

Deep fiords wind inland from the north coast of Ellesmere Island into the ice-capped interior. Once known as Grant Land after the American president Ulysses S. Grant, northern Ellesmere Island remained ice-covered until about ten thousand years ago. The ice has retreated to the interior and is divided into a large expanse to the west and a smaller one (the Grant Ice Cap) to the east; Piper Pass separates the two. Two major mountain chains, named after the British Empire and the United States, run northeast to southwest under the large ice cap and the Challenger Mountains front the north coast. Their peaks, known as *nunataks*, poke up through the ice.

Glaciers flow through a low mountain range, named after US President James Garfield, which overlooks Lake Hazen. The lake, the largest in the polar regions, lies in a "thermal oasis." Because of the orientation of the Lake Hazen basin and the melt streams flowing from the interior ice cap in summer, this remote part of Canada warms up for several months; butterflies and mosquitoes appear, snow geese settle on the lake on whose shores waves cotton grass. Arctic poppies and saxifrage colour the fringes of the *nunataks*, bringing life to these barren places. Muskoxen graze here all year round, living on dwarf willow and other vegetation. Lemmings, Peary's caribou, Arctic hares and other creatures find enough sustenance to survive the long winter.

Northern Ellesmere Island has three hundred days of winter, with the mean daily temperature below 0°C. This land is an Arctic desert. The prevailing westerly winds, blowing over the frozen Arctic Ocean, carry little moisture. The Lake Hazen basin receives between one hundred to two hundred millimetres of rain a year, the ice cap about the same amount in snow. The firn line on glaciers marks the place beyond which newly formed snow does not melt. It recrystallizes, changes into ice and adds another layer to the glacier surface.

After taking the job with the expedition, I went to Ottawa to meet its leader, Geoff Hattersley-Smith. He treated me as if I were an old Arctic hand, and his charming Greek wife Maria made me feel most welcome in their home. The Defence Research Board had sent Geoff to the north coast of Ellesmere Island in 1953 and 1954. The International Geophysical Year offered an opportunity to continue this work in a part of Canada about which almost nothing was known.

Discovering Ellesmere Island

A land may be said to be discovered the first time a European, preferably an Englishman, sets foot on it.
   – Vilhjalmur Stefansson's autobiography, *Discovery*

We can never know the names of the first discoverers of Ellesmere Island. In historic times, the Inughuit of northern Greenland called it Umingmak Island – Muskox Land – or Akalineq, the country on the other side of the sea. Recently, alarm has been expressed about these people hunting muskoxen on Ellesmere Island and threatening Canada's sovereignty. They have been doing this for years. When the Royal Canadian Mounted Police established posts on Ellesmere Island, they arrested Inughuit poachers. The Greenlanders enjoyed their stay in Canada. They and their dogs were fed and the Mounties treated them well before releasing them from comfortable prisons.

The first arrivals in northern Ellesmere Island would have given descriptive names to geographical features – here lay food caches, there was a good place to hunt muskoxen, fish could be caught in this part of the lake.

The early Inuit made no distinction between space and time. Clock time means nothing when the sun stays in the sky all day or disappears for months. The Inuit measured their journeys by the number of sleeps it took to travel from place to place. In the same way, we judged distances on the glacier and the ice cap by the time it took us to move from point to point. If I walked to the edge of the glacier, I had to make the return trip in under two hours to maintain the schedule of weather observations. A trip to the terminus of the glacier took a day – or a night. I was the sole member of the party bound by time for I had to take two-hourly observations. The others came and went at all hours of the sunlit day and night.

Around 11,000-12,000 BP (Before the Present), the High Arctic began to warm up and the ice cover on the islands retreated. Ice cores reveal that the warming trend reached its peak around 4000-5000 BP. The first people to arrive in northern Ellesmere came around 4200 BP. Known as PaleoEskimos or the Independence People (from a fiord in northern Greenland where they had established communities), these incomers may not have been Inuit. They arrived, probably from Siberia, carrying bows and arrows and wearing tailored skin clothing based on Old World patterns. They lived in dispersed settlements in the Lake Hazen basin, hunting muskoxen and hares and catching char in the lake. Around 2500 BP, these people improved their lives by building stone houses and turf structures. Around 1000 BP, they vanished, leaving meagre traces of their presence, but no memories in the minds of the next wave of settlers. Vague stories of the *tunit* – "a people earlier than ourselves" – entered Inuit folklore; they were remembered for being big and warlike.

As the climate cooled, the Thule people moved into the High Arctic. They had a highly developed culture based on hunting baleen whales in the *polynas* (open stretches of water between Ellesmere Island and Greenland). The giant mammals provided food in abundance; their bones held up the roofs of dwellings. Driftwood floated to the shores of the land and was used for buildings and sledges. During the Little Ice Age, between 1650 and 1850, ice clogged the seas and channels, driving the whales south and blocking the passage of driftwood from the Arctic Ocean. The Inuit turned to hunting land animals and seals and may have made contact with Norse traders from settlements on the coast of Greenland. The Inuit produced small works of art, sculptures in ivory, bone and wood of humans, animals and spirits. By the time they made contact with Europeans, they were in a sorry state. They had forgotten their boatbuilding skills. Ice filled the fiords, making the hunting of sea mammals very difficult. The whales had gone south and were being hunted to extinction by American and British ships.

After the end of the Napoleonic Wars in 1815, the British Navy, with a surplus of ships and seamen, took a strong interest in Arctic exploration. A famous illustration shows the first meeting of Englishmen and Inuit at Cape York in Greenland in 1818. The two naval officers in the picture, Commander John Ross and Lieutenant William Edward Parry, later gained fame as Arctic explorers. They wear cocked hats and uniforms, and carry dress swords. The fur-clad Inuit must have been astonished at how poorly equipped these newcomers were for life in the Arctic.

The British era of Arctic exploration culminated in the search for Sir John Franklin, who disappeared with his two ships and one hundred and twenty-nine men after leaving England in 1845 to search for the Northwest Passage linking the Atlantic and Pacific Oceans. As ships sailed into the northern seas, their commanders gave the names of sponsors, prominent politicians and familiar places to the lands they "discovered." Devon and Somerset Islands bear no resemblance to their namesakes. Boothia Peninsula and some High Arctic islands are named after a British gin maker (Sir Felix Booth) and Danish brewers (Amund and Ellef Ringnes). Alfred, Lord Tennyson, who married a niece of Sir John Franklin, expressed a common desire among the Victorian upper classes when he wrote: ". . . there is nothing worth living for but to have one's name inscribed on the Arctic chart."

Commander (later Admiral Sir) Edward Augustus Inglefield obliged the poet by giving his name to an Arctic feature. While searching for Franklin, this officer also sighted and named Ellesmere Island after Francis Egerton, First Earl of Ellesmere, former Secretary for War and a future president of the Royal Geographical Society. Inglefield, on the steam yacht *Isabel*, reached 78° 28' 21" N in Smith Sound in August 1852, the furthest north at that time.

The amount of ice in the waters between Ellesmere Island and Greenland varies greatly from year to year as it does elsewhere in the Arctic. Franklin picked a bad ice year when channels and straits were clogged with ice. Twenty-five years earlier, during a warm spell, William Parry took his ships through Lancaster Sound to Melville Island, where he wintered in 1819-20. He returned in triumph to Britain with a false impression of how open the Arctic was to ships. With global warming, claims are being made that soon ships will be able to traverse the Northwest Passage. As we and many others who studied the High Arctic discovered, last year's ice conditions are no guide to what happens next year.

Americans also took part in the search for Franklin. They were usually in such a hurry that they spent little time naming places. In 1854, Dr. Isaac Israel Hayes, while with the expedition of 1853-55 led by Dr. Elisha Kent Kane, crossed Smith Sound from Greenland. He saw and named Kennedy Channel to the north, Lady Franklin Bay on the coast of Ellesmere Island and Mt. Parry. Hayes named the land mass behind these features Grinnell Land after the expedition's sponsor, Henry Grinnell. The name did not take, but a mountain near Lady Franklin Bay still bears Grinnell's name.

After the search for Franklin ended in 1859, the quest to be first at the North Pole became the goal of Arctic explorers. The channel between Ellesmere Island and Greenland became known as "The American Route to the Pole." A belief arose that beyond Ellesmere and Greenland there existed the Open Polar Sea on which ships could sail to the North Pole.

In 1860, Isaac Hayes set out in the schooner *United States* for the north coast of Greenland and Grinnell Land and "to make such exploration as I might find practicable in the direction of the North Pole." He recorded a new furthest north off Lady Franklin Bay at 81° 35' N, naming the interior mountains in Ellesmere Island after his ship. In 1874, Charles Francis Hall and Sidney Budington, the sailing master of his ship *Polaris*, pushed further north, naming the body of water they crossed after Hall himself. The vessel reached 82° 11' N, from where the explorer saw a channel leading to the Arctic Ocean. He named it after George Maxwell Robeson, Secretary of the Navy, and sprinkled a few names over features on Ellesmere Island. Robeson Channel merges into the Lincoln Sea north of the island.

The British Admiralty, annoyed that the Americans had taken the lead in exploring lands claimed by Great Britain, launched its last expedition to the High Arctic in 1875. Captain (later Admiral Sir) George Strong Nares took HMS *Alert* and HMS *Discovery* through Smith Sound, hoping to reach the North Pole. Nares hit a good ice year and showed splendid seamanship. *Discovery* wintered at the harbour named after her on Lady Franklin Bay. *Alert* sailed up Robeson Channel and anchored at Floeberg Beach on northern Ellesmere Island's coast. From the frozen-in ships, exploration parties sallied overland, along the coasts and onto the ice of the Arctic Ocean.

Officers and men showed incredible grit and doggedness as they strove mightily to follow the orders issued by the Admiralty: "To attain the highest northern latitude, and, if possible, to reach the North Pole." Lieutenant (later Admiral) Pelham Aldrich determined Cape Columbia to be the most northerly point of North America, although he got its location slightly wrong. A party from *Discovery* travelled down Archer Fiord to the southwest, naming it for its leader. A sledge party under Commander (later Admiral Sir) Albert Hastings Markham headed north from Cape Joseph Henry in April 1876. As the men hauled their huge sledges, which weighed about one hundred kilograms for each man on the traces, they found themselves on a roundabout. As they headed north, the ice moved westwards. Establishing a new furthest north at 83° 20' N, the sailors, exhausted and suffering from scurvy, barely made it back to the *Alert*.

Aldrich undertook an even harder journey along the north coast of Ellesmere Island in the spring of 1876. The party advanced by a series of standing pulls – the men walked to the end of their traces, hauled the sledge forward, then repeated the task. This part of Canada has some of the worst weather in the world – I spent a summer there in 1959 – yet these British sailors did their duty, man-hauling their sledges over hundreds of kilometres of the ice shelf. Aldrich carried a thermometer slung in front of him and another hanging down his back as part of a scientific study. By the time he reached the *Alert*, only two of his men remained fit for work. With half his crews sick with scurvy, Nares headed south through the channels and basins which now collectively bear his name. They were easy to navigate, and he had no problem reaching Smith Sound.

This venture scattered one hundred and five names over northern Ellesmere Island to show that Britain exercised sovereignty there. Disraeli, Gladstone and St. Patrick had their names attached to features such as mountains, islands and bodies of water. Ward Hunt Island, at the mouth of Disraeli Fiord, owes its designation to a long-forgotten Lord of the Admiralty who served between 1874 and 1877. A story claims that Aldrich named the island, on which stands Walker Hill, because it resembled Ward Hunt lying in his bath.

The British transferred the Arctic Islands to Canada in 1880, but the new owners did nothing to assert control over them.

An American Arctic Disaster

An adventure is a sign of incompetence . . . If everything is well managed, if there are no miscalculations or mistakes, then the things that happen are only the things you expect to happen and with which you can deal.

— Vilhjalmur Stefansson

The largest American expedition to participate in the first International Polar Year set up its base at Fort Conger on Lady Franklin Bay, planning to stay in the Arctic from 1881 to 1883. The American IPY expedition – known either by the name of its leader, Lieutenant Adolphus Washington Greely, or by that of its base, Lady Franklin Bay – became the second worst disaster in the Canadian Arctic after the loss of Franklin and his men.

Greely, a member of the Fifth US Cavalry, had served in the Civil War. This brave officer, a martinet who did everything by the book, had no Arctic experience, nor did any of his men except Octave Pavy, the expedition doctor, who saw himself as an Arctic expert and resented Greely's leadership. Although the aim of the venture was to undertake scientific studies, it had another agenda – to reach a new furthest north.

The War Department organized the expedition although its head, Robert Todd Lincoln, son of the assassinated president, had no interest in scientific research or in the quest to go further north in the Arctic than anyone else. Brigadier W.B. Hazen, the Chief Signals Officer of the United States Army, had operational responsibility for the expedition. He gave Greely very specific instructions – abandon the base at Fort Conger before September 1, 1883, and sail south to meet relief ships waiting for the party north of Smith Sound. The ships would stockpile supplies on land in case the rendezvous did not take place and the expedition had to winter in the Arctic in 1883-84.

Greely named the large lake he "discovered" in the interior of Ellesmere Island after Hazen. He might have had second thoughts when he realized how badly he and his men would be let down by this officer. Almost up to the last moment there were doubts whether the expedition would leave, and the venture was marked by official procrastination, lack of support at senior levels of government and poor planning.

Greely received his command only two months before the expedition left the United States. It consisted of three officers, nineteen enlisted men, a doctor (Pavy) and two Inuit. The men, all volunteers, came from the regular army. Many had served on the western frontier; life there was considered to suit them for work and travel in the Arctic. The men appear to have been motivated by money, the search for adventure and the need to escape the boredom of barrack life on the frontier. Two men joined the expedition as specialists with the rank of sergeant. Edward Israel served as astronomer, George Rice, a Cape Bretoner, as photographer. Rice, a civilian in uniform, became well-loved for his good humour, quiet leadership and unselfish behaviour; he died seeking food for others. Some of the expedition members went north to escape demands on them. Private Henry, shot for stealing food, had killed a man and enlisted under a false name. Dr. Pavy had two wives.

The expedition ship, *Proteus*, made easy passage north in the summer of 1881 and discharged its cargo and the soldiers at Lady Franklin Bay, where they built Fort Conger. Lieutenant Kislingbury, Greely's second-in-command, was already at odds with him by the time the *Proteus* reached its destination. He resigned from the expedition and headed for the departing ship, just missing it. This tardiness cost the officer his life.

Greely's party spent two years carrying out scientific observations, exploring the coasts and interior of Ellesmere Island and seeking to establish a new furthest north in Greenland. Greely had a reputation for handling subordinates in a "fair, prudent and effective manner." His rigid personality and military-style leadership proved ill-suited to Arctic life. The men chafed in the cold, dark winter, despite Greely's attempts to alleviate their boredom. A sledge party under Lieutenant Lockwood reached 83° 24' N, about seven kilometres beyond the furthest north reached by Markham's party. Lockwood went down Archer Fiord and saw a deep inlet on the west coast of Ellesmere Island which he named after Greely.

The expedition commander made two trips inland from Fort Conger in the spring and summer of 1882. On April 30 he reached the head of the Ruggles River, the sole outlet of Lake Hazen. Greely wrote: "At 7 p.m. we were astonished beyond measure at reaching a point where the stream was open. I was inclined to doubt the evidence of my own eyes, and, indeed, rubbed them once before answering the enquiry of the men as to what it was. The open river, about fifty yards wide, and of clear water, was a rapidly running stream of an average depth of two feet."

In June, Greely led several men, dragging a cart, into the Lake Hazen basin. The cart kept breaking down and was abandoned. Making camp at the outlet of the Ruggles River, Greely found the landscape offered "a delightful and pleasant aspect . . . The sky was partly covered with true cumulus cloud . . . the sun marked with checkered bars of sunshine and shadow the bubbling river, the large blue pool . . . the temperature was high, and the gay yellow poppies and other flowers drew to them gaudy butterflies. If one but turned his back on the central ice of Lake Hazen, and the bursting glaciers from the ice-clad mountains northward of the Garfield Range, and gazed southward to the low brown hills tinged with olive-green, he could well imagine himself in the roaring forties instead of eight degrees from the geographical pole."

Greely and his companions walked along the eastern shore of Lake Hazen. On June 29, they found the weather "excessively hot, and we suffered extremely." After swinging a thermometer for seven minutes, Greely recorded the temperature as 73°F.

He then climbed Mt. Arthur, southwest of Lake Hazen, naming it for the president of the United States, struggling a kilometre through a metre of snow overlying half a metre of water. He wrote: "In my tired condition I could never have reached the top [of the mountain] except as a matter of honor and duty." Crawling on hands and knees, Greely threw his binoculars ahead of him "so as to make it certain I should proceed." He thought the mountain the highest in Grinnell Land, but it rises to only 1,295 metres.

Irving Werstein called his biography of Greely *Man Against the Elements*. The story of the officer's journey to Lake Hazen distorts the reality of the land. He claims Greely saw "[a] valley surrounded by the jutting, white cap peaks of a mountain range. Through the mist that floated over the valley [he] saw a green forest without ice and snow. Due to some climatic freak, the temperature in that valley permitted the growth of foliage and trees in an atmosphere of eternal springtime." Greely described it as "a paradise in this Arctic wilderness." Werstein reports that Sergeant Brainard, who was not with Greely, drew a map of the area while the rest of the party stood "amidst the trees [while] a gentle breeze ruffled the leaves." Forests flourished on Ellesmere Island millions of years ago, and Brainard became skilled in finding their fossilized remains.

Greely named a number of features in the interior of Ellesmere Island. The Henrietta Nesmith Glacier, west of our base camp, carries the name of his wife. The Gilman Glacier owes its name to Professor Daniel Colt Gilman, president of Johns Hopkins University, who supported the scientific work of the expedition.

A relief ship sent to Lady Franklin Bay in 1882 ran into ice blocking Kennedy Channel and stopped three hundred kilometres south of Fort Conger. The easy passage of the *Proteus* in the previous summer made the army authorities complacent. The *Neptune* landed stores and a whaleboat at Cape Sabine and sailed south. The morale of the soldiers plummetted over the winter of 1882-83. Much to Greely's dismay, Lieutenant Kislingbury played poker with the men. Dr. Pavy became even more difficult and Greely arrested him.

The expedition leader followed orders, evacuating Fort Conger on August 9, 1883. The party headed south in a steam launch towing three small boats. Had they headed for Greenland, the venture might not have ended as it did. Sergeant Cross, the only man with any knowledge of boats and seafaring, drank overmuch and proved incompetent. Greely forbade him from touching the launch's engine. Greely's behaviour became increasingly erratic as the small vessels worked their way through the ice.

When Greely and his men reached Cape Sabine on Smith Sound, they found themselves in a desperate situation. The supply ship *Proteus*, sent to pick them up, went down near Cape Sabine in July 1883, with all the supplies it carried. The expedition members would have to winter in the High Arctic with only meagre supplies, little fuel and almost no protection from the weather. Back on land, Greely's character changed. As his men starved to death, he became a considerate and compassionate leader, sometimes giving up his rations for others and doing everything possible to keep his men alive.

On June 22, 1884, Commander Schley of the United States Navy rescued the seven survivors. One had lost his hands and feet from frostbite and died on the voyage home. The Lady Franklin Bay Expedition gave the lie to the belief that big tough guys do best in the Arctic. They need more food than others; one of the smallest men with Greely, Shorty Fredericks, who survived, proved to be one of its hardiest members. Greely brought the results of his scientific observations to Starvation Camp, the first detailed information on this part of Canada. The old competitive urge emerged in his first words to his rescuers: "We have reached the Furthest North."

Greely and the five survivors received a hero's welcome on their return home. At one parade, General Benjamin Butler proclaimed, to loud applause, that Americans would not rest until they planted Old Glory at the top of the world: "The North Pole belongs to us."

Nasty rumours emerged when evidence of cannibalism appeared with the recovery of the bodies of the dead from Starvation Camp.

And there was no doubt it occurred, as it did on the Franklin Expedition. When General J.F. Weston heard of Greely's promotion to general, he snorted, "He never commanded more than ten men – and he ate three of them." However, the disaster that befell this first scientific foray into Ellesmere Island did not harm Greely's career. In 1906 he supervised relief operations during the San Francisco earthquake. In the same year, he settled a dispute with the Utes, an Indian tribe, "without a shot fired." He saw the value of new means of communication and directed the development of a telegraph system across Alaska. Greely became the mentor of Brigadier Billy Mitchell, the maverick pioneer who upset the military establishment by demonstrating how easily bombers could sink battleships; Mitchell was court martialled for insubordination and suspended from duty.

"Dolph," as Greely was called, died on October 20, 1935, at the age of ninety-two, a major general with the Congressional Medal of Honor, his nation's highest award for bravery. Throughout his long life, this officer showed courage in combat, organizational ability and imagination. All these qualities proved no match for the rigours that he and his doomed men faced in the High Arctic nor for the carelessness of those in the military who left them to starve to death at Cape Sabine.

Exercising Sovereignty

Robert Peary had one goal in life – to be the first man to reach the North Pole. Before the American did so in 1909, his Inuit hunters ranged over the Lake Hazen basin shooting muskoxen and other edible wildlife. Some of the Inuit appeared to have wintered there while Peary tore apart Fort Conger and built huts from the remains. In 1906, the American travelled along the unexplored coast of northern Ellesmere Island. On his return journey the ice began to melt and he had great difficulty reaching his base.

Peary claimed to have seen new land in the Arctic Ocean. On this coast, it is easy to be confused by anything in the distance. The explorer named his discovery Crocker Land after one of his supporters. D.B. MacMillan, who had served with Peary, tried to find this imaginary land in 1913-17 with no success.

W.E. Ekblaw, the geologist and botanist on MacMillan's expedition, reached and explored Greely Fiord in 1915, travelling with two Inughuit guides. They mapped Tanquary Fiord, naming it after the expedition's geologist. Ekblaw and his companions made an epic journey across northern Ellesmere Island, following what is now known as the Musk Ox Way from the head of Tanquary Fiord, along the shores of Lake Hazen, down the Ruggles River and Chandler Fiord to Lady Franklin Bay. The scientist named nineteen features, commemorating Arctic explorers, American biologists and geographers. Cape Macoun honours Canada's Dominion Botanist from 1882 to 1912, whose collection of flora and fauna formed the basis of the National Museum of Natural Sciences in Ottawa; it lies at the entrance to McKinley Bay, which is a tributary to Tanquary Fiord. After Operation Hazen, Geoff Hattersley-Smith submitted names for features in northern Ellesmere Island, and a lake northwest of the head of the fiord is now named after Ekblaw.

At the beginning of the twentieth century, the Canadian government became increasingly nervous about intruders into the High Arctic. In 1903, Ottawa sent Albert Peter Low, a geologist and mapmaker, to assert the nation's claim. The sealer *Neptune* took his party to Cape Herschel on Smith Sound for a Gilbert and Sullivan moment. Here "a document taking formal possession [of Ellesmere Island] in the name of Edward VII, for the Dominion, was read" then placed in a cairn. This ceremony marked Canada's first assertion of sovereignty in the High Arctic.

Between 1906 and 1911, Captain J.E. Bernier sailed the Coast Guard vessel *Arctic* around the Arctic Islands, establishing a Canadian presence there. In 1922 the Royal Canadian Mounted Police set up posts on southern Ellesmere Island and initiated the Eastern Arctic Patrol to keep tabs on intruders. In June 1929, the federal government forbade the use of "Yankee names" on lakes in the Northwest Territories, of which Ellesmere Island was a part. By this date, explorers required a permit to enter the north, where they would be under the supervision of the Mounties. One of the great unknown sagas of Canadian exploration concerns the travels made by members of the RCMP who patrolled the Arctic. Unlike the bombastic reports of men like Peary, these reports do not emphasize their sufferings in travelling long distances by dog teams under harsh conditions.

Northern Ellesmere Island remained a blank on the map for most of the first fifty years of the twentieth century, a tempting lure for the amateur explorers at the universities of Oxford and Cambridge, where clubs to encourage travel to remote places had been established in the 1920s. Journeys to the hard places of the globe such as Ellesmere Island would build character, offer physical challenges and train future leaders among the British ruling class.

In 1934, Dr. Noel Humphreys led the Oxford University Ellesmere Island Land Expedition to "the most northerly part of the British Empire." The original plan called for wintering at Fort Conger but ice prevented the expedition ship, *Signalhorn*, from reaching Lady Franklin Bay. The party spent the winter at Etah in northern Greenland.

The Inughuit taught the newcomers how to travel and live in the Arctic. Ootah, one of the three Inuit who went with Peary to what they called "The Big Nail," accompanied a party which travelled across and around southern Ellesmere Island. Ernest Shackleton's son, Edward, a member of the expedition, secured the services of RCMP Sergeant Henry Webb (Harry) Stallworthy, a seasoned Arctic traveller.

In April 1935, "the strongest party with the best Eskimos and dog teams" left Etah, the fourth venture into the interior of northern Ellesmere Island. A.W. Moore, Stallworthy, and two Inughuit – Inutuk and Nukapingua (another great Arctic traveller) – reached Fort Conger, where they found a supply depot left by Captain Godfrey Hansen in 1921 to support Roald Amundsen's plan to fly to the North Pole. The four men sledged up Black Rock Vale to the eastern end of Lake Hazen. While Stallworthy and Inutuk fished for char to feed the dogs, Moore and Nukapingua ascended the Gilman Glacier. They made their first camp – or sleep – at one thousand metres above sea level, almost at the precise spot where we established ours in 1957. Passing through the United States Range, the two travellers saw ahead of them "a great range of mountains." Moore estimated that several of the summits "must have reached ten thousand feet or more. On both flanks were a multitude of mountains, smaller than those to the north of us, and further ranges stretched as far as the eye could see."

In a burst of patriotism, Moore named his discovery the British Empire Range. The travellers climbed a nearby peak and flew the Union Jack; Moore named it after his university. Mike Marsden, an Arctic traveller who graduated from Cambridge University, confided to me his plan to sledge into the heart of northern Ellesmere Island, climb a higher mountain than Mt. Oxford and christen it "Mount Montreal High School for Girls."

Moore and Nukapingua had little time to admire the view or to travel deeper into the ice cap. With food for their dogs running short, they headed down the Gilman Glacier. (We named the pyramidical peak east of our camp and the glacier that feeds into the Gilman Glacier after Nukap.) When Moore and his companion reached Lake Hazen, they found that Stallworthy and Inutuk had caught few fish. The four men headed for Etah, reaching it on May 26, 1935.

Back in Britain, the explorers wrote books, gave lectures and spoke about their hardships and character-building sufferings. Stallworthy went back to his duties with the RCMP. This remarkable Canadian traveller received the Order of Canada in 1976, the year he died. He served much of his time in the RCMP in the Arctic, including a spell at Bache Peninsula, its most northerly post. In 1932, while searching for Dr. Hans Krüger and his party, Stallworthy sledged 2,250 kilometres around Axel Heiberg Island. The fate of Krüger remains a mystery. The northernmost tip of Axel Heiberg carries Stallworthy's name. In 2004 William Barr published his biography of the Mountie – *Red Serge & Polar Bear Pants*.

In 1939-40, a Danish expedition went up Archer Fiord to Greely Fiord, gathering information and collecting specimens. This party covered no ground that had not been previously travelled.

The first accurate maps of northern Ellesmere Island emerged from aerial photography in 1950. The limits of the ice caps and the glaciers remain vague, in part because they keep changing as they melt. Planes landed on Lake Hazen in the early 1950s – the United States Air Force put in a cache on Johns Island opposite our base camp. And doubtless the Inughuit nipped over from Greenland from time to time to shoot a few muskoxen. Operation Hazen would be the first major intrusion into this harsh, austere land.

As I read the accounts of previous expeditions to Ellesmere Island and the dangers and hardships they encountered, I wondered how I would acquit myself on Operation Hazen. We would live in tents on a glacier and I would be expected to keep records of the weather above it to complement the observations of the other scientists as we sought to unlock some of the secrets of this unknown land.

How would we fare?

How would I behave and how would I get on with the other expedition members?

These questions passed through my mind as I prepared to leave the comforts of my apartment in Montreal for three and a half months in the High Arctic.

Chapter 3

Into an Unknown Land

This was the most extreme place in North America. It drew
extreme people, nurtured extreme plants, harbored extreme
animals and showcased extreme phenomena.

> — Jerry Kobalenko, *The Horizontal Everest:*
> *Extreme Journeys on Ellesmere Island*

I had no idea who else would be on the expedition. Some of my companions trained for it on the Salmon Glacier in British Columbia. In late April 1957 I left Montreal for Ottawa to join Operation Hazen. Two friends flanked me as we walked to the train station as if accompanying a death-row inmate on his last mile. Herman, a Dutchman, thought I was crazy. Otto, my English friend, looked on my involvement with the expedition as "a bit of a lark." I had supper with female friends in Ottawa who expressed horror on learning that I would wash only my hands and face for several months.

In his introduction to *The Guinness Book of Explorers and Exploration*, Paul-Emile Victor, a seasoned polar traveller, lists the qualities of a successful explorer or adventurer. They include:

> * a bold, enterprising spirit;
> * a keen, inquiring mind;
> * a firm conviction that there are no problems, only solutions.

Other qualities include self-control ("to remain calm in any and every situation"), a sense of humour, the ability to take work seriously, but not yourself, "the ability to abandon personal pride and even self-respect," super-human patience, good health (an iron stomach and perfect teeth), an eagle eye ("always on the outlook"), and "unshakable enthusiasm and optimism, and above all, the moral fortitude to hang on and hang in . . ."

It is as well that none of us consulted such a list before joining Operation Hazen. Before leaving England I had been bothered by a pain in my lower left abdomen. A doctor dismissed it as "wind." In fact, I had a constricted urethra. On a blustery day on the glacier, when the pain came, I wrote in my diary: "Wind outside. Wind inside."

We did not have a medical examination before leaving Ottawa nor any psychological tests to determine how we would fare in the cold and isolation of northern Ellesmere Island. We volunteered in 1957 to serve as a control group for a study of one hundred and ninety-seven Bell Telephone electronic technicians who had volunteered for a one-year tour on the Mid-Canada Line. The researchers wanted to know how they would stand up under the stress of working in the north. We were shown Rorschach blots and pictures for a Thematic Appreciation Test. Keith Arnold responded to everything by saying, "It reminds me of sex." He may well have been sending up the interviewers. Most of the Rorschach blots looked like butterflies to me. One picture showed a man standing at an open window. I said that he was looking at a new day, optimistic and ready to accept any challenge it brought. We never saw the results of the study. Those on the technicians appeared in *The Journal of Applied Psychology* in 1963. The three authors concluded: "Broadly speaking . . . findings indicate that the best predictor of adjustment to an Arctic military environment is an individual's previous history of adjustment to his job and social environment."

That was certainly not the case with me.

Arctic adjustment was defined as "adequacy of overall job performance and ability to get along with other people and co-workers." After their tour of duty, each Bell technician received a performance rating from his area supervisor. The paper noted: ". . . individuals whose personalities are characterized by mood instability, restlessness, and overactivity; individuals who are inclined towards oversensitivity, reclusiveness, and emotional chal lowness; individuals whose anxieties are self-directed, as well as individuals exhibiting limited resourcefulness and capacity for dealing with stressful situations as measured by the Ego Strength scale, will experience some difficulty in making a favourable adjustment to northern isolated living."

Most of this should be pretty obvious to anyone, but the study had one interesting finding: " . . . the poorly adjusted individual feels less need for organization and orderliness, is less accepting of leadership, and shows a more critical and aggressive attitude."

Raymond Priestley in "The Polar Expedition as a Psychological Study" noted, "There are many cases of polar madness of which the world does not know." Even the Inuit, inured through centuries to cold, darkness and hardship, suffered from *pibloktog* (Arctic hysteria) but usually recovered from it. Donald MacMillan (1874-1970), an Arctic traveller, wrote of "this so-called long, dark dreary arctic night, the night that drives men mad." Royal Navy expeditions to the Arctic featured theatrical events, literacy classes, the production of newspapers, and other diversions to pass the long winter night. Officers made fools of themselves in plays, dressing up as women to boost the morale of the sailors.

Accounts of American polar ventures paint them as grim and serious undertakings. Charles Francis Hall died in November 1871, on his third attempt to reach the North Pole. Obsessed with the Arctic, this former blacksmith and newspaper publisher had a strong streak of paranoia and did not work well with others. Travelling either on his own or with a few companions, Hall made major discoveries. As an expedition leader he quarrelled with everyone and someone on his ship, the *Polaris*, slipped arsenic into his coffee. The official cause of his death was given as "apoplexy."

Greely described his men as being afflicted by "the blue devils" and experiencing depression, malaise and listlessness, which manifested themselves in "insomnia, indisposition to exertion, irritability of temper and other similar symptoms abnormal to our usual characteristics both physical and mental." The officer organized lectures to keep the minds of his men occupied and celebrated birthdays and holidays. A sense of grim seriousness, unrelieved by laughter, marked the two years Greely's expedition spent at Fort Conger.

When Richard Byrd set off to establish Little America in the Antarctic in 1928, he took with him several straitjackets and a dozen coffins. Although members of his expedition showed bizarre behaviour, including stalking, no one had to be trussed up or sent out in a coffin. On Scott's last expedition, some members regressed to their public school days, devising nicknames for their companions and engaging in horseplay. In recent years, the dark side of Scott's ventures has been exposed: Captain Oates had little time for his leader. Petty Officer Evans, a member of the party that reached the pole, must have felt like the odd man out in the company of the others, all from a different class than himself, as they struggled towards One Ton Depot. The account of Evans' death makes painful reading – he seems to have just been left to die.

Shackleton's men called him "The Boss" and most revered him. After the *Endurance* sank Shackleton kept up the morale of the party on the ice while at the same time enforcing discipline. When he told his men to discard excess baggage, he showed the way by throwing away his gold watch. Drifting on the ice, the men improvised words to familiar tunes and watched Shackleton dance stately waltzes with Frank Worsley.

Polar expeditions, like any risky, large-scale ventures, depend for their success on the calibre of the leaders. Finn Ronne, a naval officer who served with Byrd, commanded an Antarctic base and upset some of the members. They showed their disapproval of his style of leadership by pinning a dead penguin to the door of his office.

In Geoff Hattersley-Smith we had a superb leader. As he put it in typically modest fashion: "The Hazen lads largely led themselves. My role, such as it was, seemed to be jollying the lads along while dropping the occasional hint." As someone said, the people who served with Geoff returned home talking to each other. Scott sought unquestioned obedience from those under him. Amundsen secured the consent of his men before taking them into harm's way, creating an egalitarian spirit and a sense of comradeship. Geoff used the same approach.

Operation Hazen August 1958. Left to right are Keith Arnold, Barry Taylor, Dick Harington, Ian McLaren, Bob Christie, Hal Sandstrom, John Tener, Jim Lotz, Hans Weber, Dingle Smith, John Powell, Roger Deane, Jim Soper, Michel Brochu, Brian Sagar, and Geoff Hattersley-Smith.

Off To The Arctic

*The quest for the North Pole is the all-compelling instinct
to know the unknown, it matters not where. To make the
unknown known is the highest ambition of man.*

— William Wellman, an American journalist,
who failed to reach the North Pole
in 1895 and 1898

What Wellman wrote found a resonance with me. We were not
intent on reaching the pole, but we would be making the unknown
known. That unknown lay in our individual psyches – not just
in the land where we would live for months, studying its features
and its nature. The Arctic, like the world's oceans, seems endless,
unknowable, vast and overwhelming. People are drawn to them, as
Melville wrote in *Moby Dick*, by the possibility of "glimpses . . . of
some strange shore that you may visit, some land far off that holds
the answer and beauty of life." The drive to reach the North Pole
became associated with the American concept of Manifest Destiny,
a belief that the United States should rule the continent of North
America. As Peary put it, "The attainment of the North Pole is, in
my opinion, our manifest privilege and destiny."

We went to the Arctic for various reasons and were not driven
by any great urge to conquer the land or exercise dominion over the
icy wastes of northern Ellesmere Island. The land would be there
a long time after we left and we treated it with respect. Lawren
Harris, a member of the Group of Seven whose Arctic paintings
look like abstracts, claimed in 1948 that Canadians needed a "vital
experience" of their landscape to become a real nation. After my
time in the Subarctic in Schefferville, his claim had some meaning for me. It was reinforced during my time with Operation

Hazen. This venture illustrated the Canadian way of undertaking difficult tasks. It cost very little, became a collaborative enterprise and generated an enormous amount of scientific knowledge about an unknown part of Canada which we shared freely with anyone interested.

Of course, as I set out for RCAF Uplands in Ottawa in late March 1957, I had no idea how things would turn out. Geoff, Bob Christie (his companion on the ice shelf), Keith Arnold and Fraser Grant arrived a little later.

All carried large parkas and Geoff had a dog whip. I felt as I had on my first day at school. We slipped into easy familiarity and after a few days I felt as if I had known my companions for years. We boarded a North Star for the trip to Winnipeg, Manitoba, sitting along the side of the plane. In front of us lay what looked like laundry baskets; they would be packed with dog food and other supplies and dropped to us on the Gilman Glacier. Landing at Winnipeg, we saw a double rainbow and lightning flashes. Were they omens?

After a night in Winnipeg, we flew to Churchill, disembarking in a flat, snow-covered landscape. A voice shouted, "Operation Hazen people over here!" It belonged to Bert Cooney, director of the Defence Research Northern Laboratory, one of the many people who contributed to the success of Operation Hazen.

Sergeant Dave Engel joined us at Churchill. We volunteered for Operation Hazen. The Army volunteered Dave. He did not have a clue where Ellesmere Island was, but knew what he had to do – prepare an airstrip on Lake Hazen for the Flying Boxcars (also known as C-119s) that would bring in the expedition's supplies and equipment. Well-built, with a black moustache and a military bearing, this member of the Royal Canadian Engineers proved to be a rough diamond and a great boon to people with very few mechanical skills. Dave enjoyed himself so much in 1957 that he returned the following year. He swore freely and his ribald sense of humour enlivened our days on Lake Hazen. He fitted well into our small group and we treated him as a vital and important part of it.

We drew arctic gear from Army stores in Churchill, receiving clothing that included five pairs of boots and five sets of gloves. One pair of gloves, a modified mitten, had a separate finger. We puzzled over this until Dave told us it was for firing a rifle and known in the Army as "the Saturday night finger." In keeping with a long military tradition, everything was either too big or too small, fitting where it touched.

Checking the weather, we found a large high pressure system sitting over the High Arctic, giving ideal flying conditions. After a night in the Officers' Transient Quarters, at 8 a.m. Keith Arnold and I boarded a C-119, wherein sat a huge TD-9 bulldozer. Dave joined us.

We flew over Hudson Bay, which resembled a huge, shattered, frosted window pane. Leads, lines of black water, separated great sheets of ice. So little was known about the Canadian North that, for many years, it was believed the bay remained free of ice all year round. *The Ice Atlas of the Northern Hemisphere*, published in 1948, showed this. As Ken Hare, head of the Department of Geography at McGill University, said, "This struck me as absolutely preposterous." He had spoken to bush pilots who flew over the bay and reported heavily rafted and ridged ice at least a year old floating in it. At Churchill, Hare spent an evening trying to convince an Oblate missionary who had spent his life there that ice formed in the bay in winter. Vilhjalmur Stefansson, bent on proving his theory that the Arctic was a friendly place, claimed that Hare had been confused by reports of snow floating on the surface of the bay. With help from the military, Hare mounted Operation Cariberg, flying in winter in a DC-4 over Hudson Bay, making ice observations. He initiated annual flights and his students examined air movements above the bay, learning how to predict freeze-up and break-up. In 1958, while in Churchill, I heard of one ship that reached the port with its bow pushed back to its bridge after encountering the stubborn ice of Hudson Bay.

We reached Foxe, a DEW (Distant Early Warning) Line Station, at 2:20 p.m. on April 28 and had a sit-down meal of chicken and vegetables – our last for a long time. Two crashed planes sat at the end of the runway. On one of them, a truck had been improperly secured. It had broken loose on takeoff and the pilot and co-pilot had the unique distinction of being run down in the air. Climbing back into the C-119, we checked the straps holding down the big yellow bulldozer. What would happen if *that* broke loose? We asked a crew member if the plane carried parachutes. "Yes," he replied, then pointed to the white land below us. "There would be no point in bailing out – you wouldn't last a day down there." The sheer immensity of Baffin Island impressed us. Glaciers flowed from pristine, white mountains that looked ethereal and unworldly as if they belonged on a planet other than Earth. We saw bald domes, sharp peaks and deep fiords cutting into the whiteness of the island. Snow swirled over the land in strange and sinuous patterns.

Ahead of us lay the North Water, a huge, unfrozen sea that fostered the belief that it was possible to sail to the North Pole. To our right lay Greenland's icy mountains from which descended giant glaciers. The sun stayed resolutely in the sky, painting the snow surfaces with pastel shades. Everything here was on a huge scale – the land, the seas, the expanse of endless sunlit sky.

As we neared Thule Air Base in Greenland, a Scorpion fighter rose up below the C-119 and flew alongside us for a few seconds. Our pilot gave a friendly wave and the American plane slid away beneath us. We touched down at the huge base. Along the runway sat B-52s of the Strategic Air Command, huge silver bombers for delivering death to America's enemies. A jeep came up to our plane as its engines shut down and a military policeman asked to see our orders. We walked to the passenger reception centre in the corner of a huge hangar. Then we sought the toilets and encountered one of the true terrors of the Arctic. The plumbing system at Thule, designed to operate in a cold climate, flushes in a curious manner. If you did not know how to manipulate the valves on the urinals, or were not nimble enough, the system shot back at you what you had just deposited.

With Keith and Dave, I went in search of food. Finding only cold hamburger on offer at the Airmen's Mess, we returned to the reception centre, a gloomy, depressing place. We had no idea when our C-119 would take off for Lake Hazen, so I passed the time reading a pamphlet on how to become a Catholic priest – the only piece of literature in the place – and listening to the complaints of American servicemen.

Geoff had one of his rare moments of despair when he discovered that the expedition's supplies and equipment sent in advance had been scattered all over Thule. He had to hunt them down. Geoff had done a meticulous job of ordering food, supplies and equipment, based on his experience during his two summers on Ellesmere Island and his time in Antarctica. We had everything we could possibly need "except a snake-bite kit," as Geoff put it. For our first few days on the ice of Lake Hazen we would need tents, stoves, groundsheets and food. First, the airstrip would have to be bulldozed on the lake ice. Geoff asked Dave Engel and me to go in the first plane to Lake Hazen with the TD-9 bulldozer. We readily agreed.

The Flying Boxcar took off and headed across Kennedy Channel. The plane flew effortlessly over ice-choked waters through which so many explorers had struggled in their quest to reach a new furthest north. The ice caps and ranges of central Ellesmere Island came into view. We circled once and the plane made a featherlight landing on Lake Hazen. The pilots of our two Flying Boxcars from 436 RCAF Transport Command gave us the impression that landing on a lake in the High Arctic was all in a day's work. As the plane came in to land, I cast a nervous glance at the TD-9 and held on tightly to the release of my seat belt. I looked over at Dave. He sat engrossed in a paperback thriller. Like the aircrew he had no worries and we appreciated this unflappability among the service personnel who provided support for Operation Hazen.

The C-119 taxied to a halt with its engines running. The operational phase of the expedition had begun.

Dave gently eased the bulldozer out of the cargo bay of the plane and drove it clear. The propwash from the engines put a rainbow halo round the sun. The C-119 took off. Everyone involved in the landing knew we had to make haste because the weather might not hold. The second plane, carrying tents and food and the blade for the bulldozer, swooped out of the clear blue midnight sky and landed. Everyone pitched in to unload it. We attached the blade to the bulldozer without too much difficulty and set about installing a winch on the machine. Discovering that the two jacks supplied by the army to do this did not work, Dave turned the air blue with

A Royal Canadian Air Force Flying Boxcar (C-119) on Lake Hazen, April 1958. Johns Island is in the background. (National Defence photo)

Sgt. Dave Engel of the Army's Royal Canadian Engineers, attaching a winch to a tractor, Lake Hazen, May 1957. (National Defence photo)

a string of obscenities. We used a small J-5 Bombardier tractor to install the winch on the TD-9.

Dave set about clearing an airstrip for the incoming flights. An enduring memory of those early days remains: the soldier, wearing his black beret, sitting on the huge yellow machine, the only colour in this all-white landscape, doing his job, looking small and insignificant. From time to time, as we waited in the tents for the next plane to land, Dave would join us. He'd say, "Land of the Midnight Sun! Ha!" – followed by an obscenity. He expressed our sentiments admirably during those first days as we unloaded the planes and sorted out the bags, barrels, boxes and supplies.

Few accounts of polar ventures tell about those first few days of arrival which pass in a blur as you set up your camp and make sure that nothing has been left behind. The sun mocked us with its lack of warmth as the temperature hovered between -20° and -30°C. The cold seeped into our bones and brains and stayed there, numbing us, making clumsy every movement. We pitched our tents on the ice between Johns Island and the site of the base camp on the north shore of Lake Hazen. They were of the same design as those used by Scott in the Antarctic, pyramid shaped with double walls that did not keep out the cold. Two-burner Coleman stoves warmed the tents and were used for cooking. We put them out when we left the tents and had to relight them with frozen fingers when we returned.

In theory, pyramid tents hug the surface more closely when the wind blows: the stronger the wind, the more stable the tents would become. I noted a rope hanging from the apex of a tent and asked Geoff the reason for it. "You hang on to it if the wind gets under the skirts of the tent and it begins to blow away," he replied. "That happened in Antarctica." Bob Christie suggested we could hang the stoves from the rope when the melt season began

Pyramid tents on the Gilman Glacier. Mount Nukap is in the background. (National Defence photo)

and the tents became waterlogged. Geoff and Bob had erected the tents. On top of a groundsheet they laid caribou skins, which have numerous tiny, hollow fibres that insulate the animals from the cold. Our double army-issue sleeping bags went on top of the skins and we slept in our parkas and windpants. The cold of the lake ice lanced up through the various layers and hit our bodies like knives, making sleep difficult.

Just as we fell into an uneasy doze, the cry went up, "Plane!" Grabbing snow goggles and gloves, we fell out of the circular tent opening, staggered over to a C-119 and unloaded it. Night and day became meaningless words as we lost any sense of time. We ate and slept when we could. Hunkered down in our sleeping bags, we missed the spectacular sight of an Arctic solar eclipse. We cared nothing for such wonders. We craved only sleep and warmth and had precious little of either. I began to regret my decision to join Operation Hazen. Nothing I had read about polar exploration had prepared me for the sheer bloody hard work at the beginning of an expedition. But there was no going back – I was committed and could not let down the others. Walking, which resembled slogging through fine sand, exhausted me; I had to drag each foot forward and make an effort to keep going. Staggering around bleary-eyed, carrying boxes and bags, pushing barrels, hauling bits and pieces from the cargo bays of the C-119s, I had no time to wonder at the beauty of this Arctic Eden.

Ten airlifts brought in thirty-five tons for the expedition's first summer. An RCAF survey crew arrived, built a hut, erected a tower on Johns Island and set about their work. Keith and I walked up the hill to greet them, envying the luxury of their snug accommodation, the fresh eggs, vegetables and other delicacies they enjoyed – and the fact that they would be back home in a week or so. Roger Deane and Bob Christie, who would spend the summer at the base camp, erected a hut on the shore of Lake Hazen.

Finally, the C-119 flights ended and all our supplies and gear lay, neatly stacked, on the ice of the lake. We began to sort out stuff and to move part of it to the base camp.

On May 3, a DC-3 of Air Transport Command (ATC) touched down on the lake. From it emerged three senior RCAF officers: Air Vice Marshal Bryons, head of ATC, Air Commodore Carpenter and Group Captain Schroeder. In my two years in the Royal Air Force, I had never seen so much high-priced help in one place at one time. The three officers arrived to supervise the work that had already been done – and for a photo opportunity. We lined up for the photographer then flew to the Gilman Glacier.

The main camp of Operation Hazen on the north shore of Lake Hazen. (RCAF photo)

Trevor Harwood had carried out a reconnaissance in the spring of 1956 in a DC-3 piloted by Wing Commander J.G. "Jack" Showler, a little-known Arctic air pioneer from 408 Squadron. They had landed the plane on Lake Hazen without difficulty and other planes had set down on the lake ice, but whether a fully-loaded C-119 could do so was unknown, until that first landing with the bulldozer. Showler took the plane up the Gilman Glacier and landed it at a thousand metres above sea level — the first time this had been done in Canada. Harwood got out, wearing a parka over his business suit, surveyed the site and decided that we should place our glacier camp there. It lay about two or three kilometres from the sides of the glacier, fourteen kilometres from its terminus and six kilometres from where it merged into the ice cap. Our camp would be located at a critical point on the ice, in the melt zone. We could determine what happened when the weather warmed up and also have access to the permanent ice that never melted during the summer.

The RCAF officers pitched in, helping us to unload the DC-3 on the glacier. I saw a hooded figure manhandling a box inside the plane. "Mind my bloody instruments — they're in that crate!" I shouted. A very abashed air vice marshal carefully handed me the box. Rank and status have no privilege in the Arctic; everyone has to help when time is pressing. If you screw up, you are promptly told about it. A mistake can imperil your companions, damage or smash a vital piece of equipment, ruin the whole enterprise. Rigid, authoritarian, hierarchical systems based on the command and control model do not work in extreme situations. On Operation Hazen, we became spokes in a wheel at whose hub stood Geoff Hattersley-Smith. The support staff formed the rim that kept us in contact with the various bits and pieces that made up the enterprise; they provided the expertise we lacked when we needed it, where we needed it.

A Royal Canadian Air Force ski-wheel DC-3 (also known as a Dakota) establishing the camp on the Gilman Glacier, May 1957. (National Defence photo)

The DC-3 left, carrying Geoff and the officers. Fraser Grant and I were expected to erect the tents on the glacier.

I looked at him and he looked at me.

It was obvious that neither he nor I knew how to erect a pyramid tent on a glacier. We took the tent out of its bag, held it upright, and spread the two front poles. We dug them into the ice and tried to do the same with the two rear poles. The tent collapsed. We dug in the two front poles. Again the tent collapsed.

After much fumbling, we had the tents up and placed boxes of human and dog food on the skirts to anchor them. We threw caribou skins, Coleman stoves, spare clothing, ration boxes, pots and pans and other bits and pieces into each tent. The dogs arrived on the next DC-3 flight.

"Make ice anchors to hold them," Geoff said.

The blank expression on my face told him this was another skill I lacked.

Grabbing an ice chisel, Geoff dug two parallel trenches in the ice. Wielding an ice axe, he connected them, explaining, "The

A DC-3 sits behind a pyramid tent on the Gilman Glacier, May 1958. The tent had stood all winter. (National Defence photo)

traces go through that hole." Vainly trying to do as he did, I botched the job. Digging two trenches with an ice chisel proved easy. The difficult bit involved connecting them. Either I would smash the ice surface with my clumsy use of the ice axe or the anchor would come apart when I threaded the traces through it. Geoff looked at my handiwork and said, "We'll figure out another way of tethering the dogs. The ice here must be very brittle."

Cloud moved in as the Flying Boxcars roared down the glacier, paradropping the panniers containing dog food and other supplies. AVM Bryons grabbed the radio mike as the chutes came down, complaining to the pilots about the drop. We had no objections – this was an easier way of securing our supplies than hauling them up by sledge from the base camp.

The DC-3 left about three in the morning. Retrieving some of the baskets, we emptied them and stacked others in front of the tents. We had shelter, food, fuel for the stoves on which we could cook and our sleeping bags. We knew we would survive in this harsh, empty land. So we decided to get some sleep as the calm weather persisted. After a few hours, we arose and brought in the rest of the air drop, with the help – and hindrance – of the dogs. The snow surface on the glacier differed markedly from that on Lake Hazen, with firm patches alternating with soft ones. In places, the crust suddenly gave way and I floundered in the snow. I'd step on a soft patch and almost fall flat on my face.

The military used Operation Hazen to test some new equipment, including a magnesium toboggan called a *pulka*. I hauled a basket on to one of them and tried to pull it. The friction of the snow made this difficult and the pannier kept falling off the *pulka*. This man-hauled sledge would be of limited use in the Arctic. The dogs proved equally unsuited to the work we assigned them. Frisky and happy to be in a place that resembled home – they came from Kanaq in Greenland – the animals showed no interest in helping us when we tried to tie them to the baskets. So we resorted to sliding the panniers along by hand, recovering every one just as the wind rose, clouds filled the sky, and loose snow moved over the glacier surface.

"Looks like a blizzard," said Geoff.

The four of us – Geoff, Fraser, Keith and myself – crowded into one tent as the wind hurled loose snow against its walls, and examined the harnesses that had come with the dogs. Made of sealskin, they were tattered and torn and would be useless when the time came to hitch the dogs to sledges; the traces, also made of sealskin, were in good shape. We made new harnesses for the animals from the parachute straps. It took eight hours to make each one. Pushing needles through the stubborn nylon, we discussed the summer's work. I would have to stay at the glacier camp, reading the instruments measuring the weather above the ice surface.

Geoff, Fraser and Keith had to decide how best to use their three and a half months on the ice.

"Should we concentrate our efforts on the Gilman or travel in the interior ice cap?" Geoff asked. The tension between scientific studies and the lure of exploring unknown lands emerges in many narratives of polar expeditions. We opted for an intensive study of the Gilman Glacier.

Operation Hazen had a number of goals, including establishing Canadian sovereignty in the High Arctic. Geoff's main concern was to determine the mass balance of the Gilman Glacier. This would give some indication of what was happening to other glaciers and ice masses in northern Ellesmere Island. In June, two assistants for Fraser Grant – Hal Sandstrom and John Filo – would join us, making up a team of six for the study of the glacier.

The wind continued to rise. Snow snaked down the glacier surface, rattling louder and louder against the rear wall of the tent. From time to time, Geoff stuck his head out of the tent door. A blizzard is defined as a period of wind during which, no matter in which direction you pee, it comes back and hits you. Geoff used graphic language to describe the whiteness that surrounded our tents: "Like being inside a ping-pong ball. Rather less than ten percent of minus bugger-all out there."

The blizzard lasted through the day and night and into the following day. We sallied out from time to time for a quick pee, then hastened back to the warmth of the tents. The dogs snuggled down, nose to tail, quite at home in this weather. Inside the tents we talked of many things and drank lots of tea. Cosy and warm in our small world, we relaxed and prepared meals in leisurely fashion. I shared a tent with Keith, but we joined Geoff and Fraser in theirs for meals to save fuel. We wondered whether our summer would be one of blizzards like this, but the Big Blow of early May proved to be the only one during the two summers.

My feelings about the expedition changed.

I had an itchy beard. My filthy clothes had not been changed in a week. My left shoulder pained me and a strip across the base of my spine felt permanently frozen. And I felt great. My romantic notions about life on an Arctic expedition had not been dented by reality. Feelings of contentment increased as we crawled out of the tents when the blizzard ended and looked around us.

The scenery held us breathless.

To the east rose a mountain peak shaped like a pyramid.

To the west lay a large mountain mass resembling the statue of Lincoln in his memorial in Washington. From the snow-covered central peak stretched out two ridges resembling arms. The utter serenity and silence of the place lifted our spirits while making us aware of our own puny insignificance in this remote land where only two men had been before us.

Down-glacier we could not see Lake Hazen, hidden in its basin. Beyond it rose the Agassiz Ice Cap at the head of Archer Fiord. First things first, we decided. We blew a hole in the ice well below the tents, took the top off an oil drum and put it in the cavity. On top of the drum we placed a basket with a caribou skin over it. Cutting a hole in the skin and the basket we had a toilet with a magnificent view.

Up-glacier stood the mountains of the British Empire Range. From time to time we saw great swirls of snow there, looking like white giants in combat.

After a few minutes of simply staring at the landscape, now covered in new snow from the blizzard, we began to dig out our buried supplies and equipment and put the camp in order. The campsite looked like an archeological dig as we trenched the snow.

Geoff gave us his perspective on the blizzard: "It wasn't too bad. No one had to shit in the tent."

Brian Sagar on the Gilman Glacier with Mount Nukap in the background and the pyramid tent camp on the right.

Chapter 4

Companions – Human

In the Arctic, one's job is accomplished against a background of continual struggle for existence. A great deal depends on the individual. If he gives less than his best he is finished, and his failure may be fatal to the men in his outfit as well as himself.

— Peter Freuchen (1886-1957)

We never lived under such harsh conditions as did Freuchen, a legendary Arctic traveller. His observation rings true for those who have had to cope with the Great Outdoors and the Little Indoors in extreme parts of the world. Isolation and hardship sharpen the edges of some people, dull those of others. Individuals become more like what they really are – more petty, more generous, more cowardly, braver than in the everyday world. It's as if the Arctic becomes a huge magnifying glass through which you see, more clearly than in the crowded south, your weaknesses and strengths. Greely came apart on the retreat in 1883 from Fort Conger while George Rice, the expedition's photographer, emerged as a leader, continually concerned with the survival of his companions, forever cheerful, risking his life for others.

Military discipline failed to create a sense of comradeship on Greely's Arctic venture. On Operation Hazen, a sense of easy and unforced friendship emerged very quickly. Everyone pitched in when someone else needed a hand, taking turns at the muscle-wrenching task of coring ice by hand and re-erecting the meteorological mast when it collapsed. Geoff assumed that we knew our jobs and let us get on with them. I recall only one quarrel during the two summers. At the end of the 1957 season, Keith wanted to use the radio to send a message to his wife. I had charge of the radio and insisted that we retain the remaining power in the batteries to communicate with the base camp.

Jonathan Karpoff published a paper in the February 2001 issue of the *Journal of Political Economy* entitled "Public Versus Private Initiative in Arctic Exploration: The Effects of Incentives and Organizational Structure." He examined records from ninety-two Arctic expeditions between 1818 and 1909, finding that publicly funded ones had "significantly worse outcomes that privately financed ones." He concluded that the reason for the success of the latter was because they were led by organizers in seventy-eight percent of cases. Only twenty-seven percent of government-funded endeavours had this kind of leadership. According to Karpoff, "Because they did not actually go on trips, the organizers of public expeditions faced few of the negative consequences of poor planning or erroneous theories."

Errors included misguided views on proper clothing, scurvy prevention, optimal travel modes and the existence of the fictitious Open Polar Sea. Operation Hazen refuted this theory for it was publicly funded by the Defence Research Board. The 1959 Ice Shelf Expedition confirmed Karpoff's theory; it was organized by the United States Air Force. My time with the Canadian venture still shines in my memory. My involvement with the American expedition left a residue of ill-feeling, fueled in part by the death of my good friend Paul Walker.

Human Dynamics in the Arctic

In his poem "Men of the High North," Robert Service described them as "steel-braced, straight-lipped, enduring / Dreadless in danger and dire in defeat."

This image obscures the reality of expedition life in the polar regions. Good planning and organization are required for a successful venture and outstanding leadership is vital. But the dynamics of human interaction in cold climates has its own peculiarities that cannot be foretold. Those who join expeditions are inevitably risk-takers. But all have their limits and this becomes readily apparent in extreme situations. Weldy Phipps, a pioneer Arctic flyer who developed balloon tires that made landing in unlikely places possible, noted: "Know your limits and those of your equipment and never exceed either."

In *Leading at the Edge: Leadership Lessons from the Extraordinary Saga of Shackleton's Antarctic Expedition*, Dennis Perkins, a former American Marine officer turned management consultant, contrasts the leadership styles of Shackleton, Stefansson and Scott. He finds Stef too individualistic, prone to go off on his own, and an avid self-promoter. Scott, at the other end of the management spectrum, rigid, insecure, a terrible communicator, had the crew of the *Discovery* scrubbing its decks in freezing weather. Shackleton emphasized team work, self-sacrifice and courtesy. He served in the Merchant Navy where relationships between officers and men were much more informal than in the Royal Navy, which nurtured Scott's style of leadership. Shackleton could have reached the South Pole in 1909 – had he been willing to sacrifice his own life and those of his comrades.

When disaster strikes a polar venture, it's difficult to tell how its members will behave, even with the sort of leadership that Shackleton demonstrated. Thomas Orde Lees, a Royal Marine Officer seconded to the *Endurance* expedition, took charge of the supplies while the party drifted on the ice after the ship sank. Nicknamed "The Colonel" by others and "The Old Maid" by Shackleton, he was seen as a liability. A busybody, given to excessive chatter, he was viewed by Shackleton as too rational, too reasonable, too worried about whether the supplies would last. Lees' concern for the security and safety of others appeared when he served in the Royal Flying Corps during the First World War; he pestered senior officers to equip pilots with parachutes.

John Vincent, the ship's bosun, proved to be a bully. After drifting in the ice, the party landed on Elephant Island. Taking a small boat, the *James Caird*, Shackleton set out to reach South Georgia, where there was a whaling station. He took Vincent with him, for two reasons – leaving him on the island might have proved bad for the morale of the others and the bosun, as one of the strongest men in the party, would be tough enough to handle life in a small boat as it ploughed through rough seas. Instead, Vincent collapsed, physically and mentally, during the epic voyage to South Georgia.

Shackleton, a larger-than-life figure who "lived like a mighty rushing wind" in the words of a friend, played the role of the polar explorer to the hilt in order to raise money for his expeditions. But his success depended on men like Frank Wild and Frank Worsley. The latter captained the *Endurance* and navigated the *James Caird* across some of the worst seas in the world. Wild undertook one of the greatest sledge journeys in Antarctica with Shackleton, reaching a point one hundred and eighty kilometres from the pole.

While with the Department of Northern Affairs and National Resources in Ottawa, I shared an office with Dr. Diamond Jenness, the anthropologist on the 1913-16 Canadian Arctic Expedition. Led by Stefansson, it set forth in 1913 and ended in disaster. To the end of his days, Dr. Jenness would not talk about his time with the venture. R.W. Anderson, the scientific leader, was constantly at odds with Stef, who wanted to find new lands in the Arctic. Stef left the expedition ship, HMCS *Karluk*, before it sank north of Wrangel Island in January 1914. Captain Bob Bartlett, the legendary Newfoundland sailor and explorer, walked 1,100 kilometres to Russia to find help for the stranded crew.

William Laird McKinlay, the magnetician, kept quiet about his experiences on the expedition for sixty years. He claimed that the crew of the *Karluk* became "a band of self-interested individuals. Lying, cheating and stealing became common behaviour." In *Karluk*, published in 1976, McKinlay compared his time in the Arctic with his experiences as an officer with the 51st Highland Division during the First World War: "The loyalty, the comradeship, the *esprit de corps* of my fellow officers and of the men it was my privilege to command enabled us to survive the horrors of war, and I realized that this was what had been entirely missing up north: it was the lack of real comradeship that had left the scars, not the physical rigours and hazards of the ice pack, nor the deprivation on Wrangel Island." Anyone interested in the CAE or Jenness, a Canadian pioneer anthropologist, should read McKinlay's *Karluk: The Great Untold Story of Arctic Exploration*, Jennifer Niven's *The Ice Master: The Doomed 1913 Voyage of the Karluk,* or Harold Horwood's *Bartlett, The Great Explorer.*

In recent years, those who set out into the polar regions do so to show how hardy, brave and strong they are – or to demonstrate their commitment to a cause. Their clothing and gear often covered in endorsements, they attract media attention when they leave and on their return when they write a book about their exploits. Some of the dafter polar ventures are rationalized by claiming they involve studies of human endurance in extreme cold. This can be more accurately assessed in specially built test chambers. Some pole vaulters see their feats as a way of inspiring young people and creating environmental awareness. Robert Swan reached both poles. In *Icewalk,* he listed the reasons for doing so:

> The cold.
>
> Getting to the Pole.
>
> My valiant friends.
>
> Because it is cold.
>
> Because we can do it.
>
> Because we can do something with it.
>
> Because nobody has ever done it.
>
> Because I'll never do it again.

None of these reasons makes much sense, but they are well in line with the illogicality that has marked so many polar ventures in the past, especially those carried out by British people who go to the poles "because they are there."

These days, few northern ventures in Canada are launched without being rationalized as studies of global warming. The Arctic, seen like a canary in a coal mine, serves as an early warning line for what might happen elsewhere as the climate warms up. Time in the north, however, has value in two areas of human organization. What happens when people are crammed together in small spaces in cold climates offers some indication of how they will act on space voyages. Studies of polar ventures are also useful in identifying how teams operate under conditions of stress. One small mistake in the north – and in a large enterprise – can have disastrous results.

In *The Devil's Labyrinth*, Clive Johnson tells how an error in judgement doomed his attempt to walk to the North Pole in 1994. On the seventh day on the ice, he removed his outer gloves to take photos and froze his fingers. After two and a half more weeks, the party discovered it had moved only one degree north – about one hundred and twenty kilometres – from its starting point because of the circular motion of ice in the Arctic Ocean. Johnson's painful fingers needed medical attention. The three men camped on the ice and sent for a plane. Russian rescuers held the stranded men to ransom, demanding an exorbitant sum to pick them up. The explorers found the money and were taken to safety. The action of the Russians went against the grain of the Arctic tradition of selfless action when disaster strikes: Amundsen lost his life in 1928 while searching for the downed airship *Italia*.

I made my first mistake on Operation Hazen a day or two after we arrived. We stuck a knife in the snow outside the tent. When someone asked for it, I did not want to enter the tent waving it around, possibly piercing someone in the crowded quarters. So I stuck it, pirate-fashion, in my mouth. The icy metal removed skin from my lips and tongue.

Cultures have different ways of dealing with isolation and hardship. A friend travelled with an Inuk, becoming storm-stayed in a blizzard in an igloo. He wondered and worried while his companion appeared calm. "What are you thinking about?" he asked. "Nothing," came the reply.

Polar Bridge, a joint thirteen-man Canadian-Soviet expedition, set out in 1988 to travel from northern Siberia to Ellesmere Island, and to demonstrate international solidarity while doing so. This venture achieved the first goal – but not the second one. Crossing the Arctic Ocean on skis and on foot, the members argued and disagreed with each other about almost every aspect of northern travel. The Canadians filled their diaries with details of suffering, illness and discord with their fellow countrymen and with the Russians, wondering why they had become involved in such a foolhardy undertaking. At one stage, members of the expedition did not speak to each other for days. What Canadians saw as violent verbal arguments among the Russians they dismissed as "a discussion."

A Canadian received a cake from his wife; he ate some at lunch breaks, trading chunks of it with a fellow traveller for chocolate. A Russian echoed the sentiments of his colleagues: "If I had a cake from my wife, I would share it with everyone." The Canadian replied that his wife "had made [the cake] for me. She didn't make it for anyone else."

After a while in isolation in the hard places of the earth, small and petty matters become major irritants. The way a companion blows his nose or scratches his backside or mumbles in his sleep plays on your nerves and you think evil thoughts about him. With others, you feel an immediate bond of fellowship and anything they do, no matter how annoying, is alright. Cliques often form on large polar ventures, but we avoided this on Operation Hazen. Richard Weber, son of Hans Weber (who was with us on the glacier in 1958), hit it off with Mikhail Malakhov, a Russian, on the Polar Bridge Expedition. They decided to go to the pole in 1992 and invited Bob Mantell, an American, to join them.

On the thirty-fifth day on the ice, Mantell took the lead, walking so rapidly that his companions could scarcely keep up with him. At the next rest stop, the American said, "Guys, I need to talk about leaving the expedition. I'm going to make my own way to Ward Hunt Island." One of the current mystiques in polar travel these days revolves around the idea of expeditions having an "unsupported status." You carry everything you need with you to the poles and don't rely on airdrops or supply planes landing near you. Malakhov agreed that Mantell should walk back to Ward Hunt Island to maintain the unsupported status of the expedition. The American lost his way; it took a four-day air search to locate and rescue him. On their ninety-first day on the ice Weber and Malakhov reached their limits and asked to be picked up. They tried again in 1995. Leaving in February, and travelling unsupported, they reached the pole and returned safely.

The Curious Nature of Polar Expeditions

The worst part of a polar expedition is over when preparation has ended and the journey begun.

— Fridtjof Nansen (1861-1930)

Ventures to the Arctic and Antarctic bring together diverse people for a brief period. These individuals may not have much in common, but the chemistry between them is vital to the venture's success. Geoff had no way of knowing how we would work together. He had gone to northern Ellesmere Island in 1953 with a geologist and two Inughuit. In the following year, he led a party of four.

On Operation Hazen, we all came from different settings and Geoff had no say in hiring some of us. He worked for the Defence Research Board and Bob Christie for the Geological Survey of Canada. DRB contracted with McGill University to supply a glacial meteorologist (me) in the summer of 1957 and four weather observers to winter over at Lake Hazen in 1957-58. Roger Deane, Fraser Grant, John Filo, Hal Sandstrom and Keith Arnold came under contract with the University of Toronto.

In 1958, government departments were invited to participate in Operation Hazen and several sent representatives to do field work. We did our own thing and shared what we learned with each other – and then parted. I returned with Geoff for three weeks in 1960, living on the Gilman and travelling around the ice cap. It proved easier to approach northern Ellesmere Island via Tanquary Fiord, so in 1962 Operation Hazen became Operation Tanquary. It lasted until 1970 and involved about eighty scientists. Then this phase of scientific research in the High Arctic ended. Such ventures move from being very diffuse – in 1957 we had to determine some of the dimensions of the island and its problems – to focusing on certain aspects of the environment that scientists consider more worthy of study. Since 1970, visitors to northern Ellesmere Island have climbed mountains and travelled around the lowland parts of the area. But there has been no ongoing scientific research program like the one initiated by Operation Hazen in 1957.

Three remarkable men planned and organized the expedition. Frank Davies, born in Merthyr Tydfil, Wales, came to Canada as a lecturer in physics at the University of Saskatchewan in 1925, moving to McGill University in the following year. He joined the 1928 Byrd Expedition, wintering over in Little America. This venture had a sharp distinction between officers and men. Davies served as a bridge between them, eating with the men. His genial personality and fine sense of humour made him popular among the Americans. In 1932-33, Davies led a four-man expedition to Chesterfield Inlet to carry out meteorological, geomagnetic and auroral studies as part of the Second International Polar Year. He masterminded and championed Canada's contribution to the International Geophysical Year as director of the Defence Research Board. Bluff, informal and plain-spoken, he had the knack of putting people at ease.

An incident in his life reveals the kind of man Frank Davies was. At Little America, the latrine consisted of a trench in the snow with a wooden bench with a seat above it. Someone rigged the seat in the "Crystal Palace" with a charge of flash powder. It exploded when the seat was lowered – much to Davies' surprise. He took the prank in good spirit, but always remembered the comfort needs of those who went on polar expeditions. He visited the Tanquary camp in 1968 and decided to upgrade its facilities. Later in the season, a splendid toilet he designed arrived at the camp by icebreaker

Davies left the organization and direction of Operation Hazen to Trevor Harwood and Geoff Hattersley-Smith, two markedly different individuals. Bald-headed, strongly built, Trevor Harwood's feats and language marked him as a unique individual in Canada's military bureaucracy. When I first met him in 1954, he headed the Defence Research Board's Arctic Section. It operated from a small suite of bare-bones offices in the temporary buildings opposite the Lord Elgin Hotel in Ottawa; it was later renamed the Geophysics Section.

Harwood was born in Darlington, England, in 1914, a place he heartily disliked. The Harwood family arrived in Montreal in 1928 and Trevor soon showed his adventurous nature by shipping as a cabin boy on a vessel sailing from Boston to Australia while still in school. At the age of twenty, he joined the Hudson's Bay Company, claiming to have mistaken the annual salary for a monthly one. Harwood spent five years with the HBC, two of them at Dundas Harbour on Devon Island where the RCMP had a detachment.

Harwood travelled extensively in the Arctic, crossing the Devon Island ice cap from Dundas Harbour to Craig Harbour on southern Ellesmere Island, then spending three years at the HBC post at Pangnirtung on Baffin Island. Saving his money while in the Arctic, Harwood enrolled in the University of Toronto in 1939, leaving after a year to join the Royal Canadian Navy. He served in the North Atlantic, the Mediterranean and in the invasion of Normandy. Demobilized as a lieutenant-commander, Harwood went back to university, graduating with a degree in geology in 1949, then joined DRB's Arctic Section. In the following year he circumnavigated Cornwallis Island by canoe with two companions, carrying out a geological reconnaissance.

At Resolute he held a group of listeners spellbound with his unique method of explaining the subtleties of the language of the Inuit: "If you say you are going for a piss in Inuktitut, and you mean sometime in the future, that's one word. If you say you're going in an hour or two, that another word. But if you dash out of the room with your dick in your hand shouting, I'm going for a piss! – that's *another* word."

Harwood picked up another habit from the Inuit with whom he traded. If you started a conversation with him and had to break it off, he would continue it months or years later. He had a forceful way with language. Once, while I was talking with Geoff in his office, Harwood walked in, said, "You'll have to whatsisname" and walked out. When Geoff returned from educational leave after completing his DPhil at Oxford University in 1956, as he put it: "I was told by our gallant commander to get off my arse and organize [Operation Hazen]."

Harwood went by a variety of titles, including "Curious." He had an amazing store of arcane knowledge, once telling me how to bypass the Iron Curtain and travel to East Germany by claiming to have property there. Harwood had the habit of helping himself to other people's cigarettes. One day, a colleague ground up a pencil eraser and replaced the tobacco in a cigarette with it. Harwood came into his office, picked up the cigarette, lit it and puffed away, wanting to know, "What's that Christly smell?"

Harwood became an expert at "skunk work," at getting things done in unorthodox ways. He recognized that if you are going to do unconventional things in a bureaucracy you have to dress in conventional ways, so he always wore a grey suit. He treated everyone equally and never deferred to rank or authority. Fortunately, his superiors in DRB recognized his peculiar talents and skills and allowed him plenty of leeway. A former board chairman noted, "If I wanted something done in a hurry, I gave it to the Geophysics Section but asked no questions as to how it would be done." Harwood believed that there were more ways than one to skin a cat – a favourite expression.

Skilled at cutting through red tape, he knew how to bypass or subvert normal bureaucratic channels. He worried about the people on the expedition and we paid tribute to him by naming a husky after him. One day, Martha, the secretary of the McGill Geography Department, received a phone call from Harwood. In typically brusque fashion, he demanded, "How much are we paying Lotz?"

"$300 a month," Martha replied. Harwood harrumphed and rang off, and later I learned that my salary had gone up to $430.

Underneath, Harwood nurtured a sensitive soul. As Geoff said, "If a few were put off by his often brusque manner, they knew not the kindly heart and essentially shy personality that lay beneath it."

Our field leader presented a complete contrast to Harwood. If Trevor gave the impression of pushing forcefully into the wind and battling the elements, Geoff Hattersley-Smith seemed always to be leaning back into the wind, comfortable, relaxed and unfazed by anything. Tall, lean, with an abstracted air at times, Geoff sometimes sounded apologetic in conversation. He epitomized the English tradition of blending an urge for adventure and a desire to visit unknown lands with sound scientific training and a mind attuned to probing the earth's mysteries. Geoff travelled with Tom Manning, who turned his back on the family fortune and explored the Arctic, carrying out scientific research on the wildlife and eating anything that came his way. According to Geoff, "His igloo or tent was no place for the squeamish, for there was no difference between the culinary and the zoological arrangements." Geoff travelled hard and lived on basic foods. But, as he put it, "I was no explorer, nor ever reduced to the extremity of eating 'the friend of man.'" He asked Manning what dog tasted like and was told, "I prefer it to wolf."

Geoff had the gift of all good leaders – that of affirmation; he always made us feel competent in what we were doing, even when we fumbled around. In 1949-50, while with the British Antarctic Survey, he served as glaciologist and base leader on King George Island in the South Shetlands. He travelled extensively on King

Geoff Hattersley-Smith

George Island, a place noted for its ferocious weather and rugged and crevassed terrain. Of this experience, he noted, "I became cautious, probably overcautious." Joining the Defence Research Board in 1951, he carried out research in the Yukon, the Beaufort Sea and Cornwallis Island and led Canadian-US expeditions to the northern coast of Ellesmere Island in 1953 and 1954.

During the Second World War, Geoff served on a destroyer escort guarding freighters on the hazardous run to Murmansk in northern Russia. This experience gave him a standard by which he judged his time in the polar regions. He said of Operation Hazen: "I tended to regard the whole business as a continuation of the same job, having served previously on the north coast, and before that, in the Antarctic, which had seemed like a piece of cake compared to the Russian convoys, on which U-boats could be quite tiresome."

We had complete confidence in Geoff, who never gave a direct order. In 1958, however, he circulated a memo that we all had to sign. On the ice shelf expedition in 1954, he lost contact with Bob Christie and a companion as the melt season began. Wading through slush and standing water in M'Clintock Inlet, he spotted the two men, later writing: "The very awkward situation that could have been caused by the sudden and unexpected onset of the melt season was thus averted."

Geoff's 1958 memo stated: "[The] safety of each and every member of the group is paramount and thus it is necessary to lay down very clear and definite terms detailing responsibility. Since the lake party will be separated into small parties it is necessary to delegate clear cut authority at the main camp on matters affecting the operation as a whole and the safety of its members."

Roger Deane served as leader at the lake camp, with Bob Christie as his deputy. The memo continued: "No person will be away from the main camp more than twenty-four hours without a companion. Before field trips all parties will leave a written itinerary at base camp signed by the party leader, giving their latest date of return . . . Many of the rivers are treacherous in the melt season . . . The largest streams must not be crossed by a lone person . . . At river crossings packs should be worn with one shoulder strap only, so that the pack can be discarded if necessary. Ropes, ice-axes and crampons will be carried on all journeys involving glacier travel."

Even at his most easygoing, you sensed the steel under Geoff's relaxed behaviour. I only saw him lose his cool on a few occasions when dogs dragged him down-glacier. He cursed them with great vigour until he regained control. Geoff led from the rear, in a non-directive manner. On a trip down-glacier, we had to cross a deep channel along which icy water swirled. Before leaping nimbly across it, Geoff cautioned me: "If you fall into that, there's nothing I can do to save you." I made the leap safely.

Dick Harington, leader of the winter party at the lake, took solitary walks in the surrounding countryside, returning from one with a badly frozen toe. Dick visited the glacier camp during the summer of 1958. Strapping on his skis one evening, he said he was heading up-glacier "just to have a look around." When he had not returned to our camp by early morning, Geoff roused me from my sleep. We piled food, clothing, ropes and a tent on a sledge. Crevasses formed at the head of the glacier and Dick might have fallen into one of them. Hitching the sledge to a snowmobile, we followed Dick's ski tracks towards the ice cap. After three freezing hours, we saw Dick ahead of us, still moving forward. As we reached him, all Geoff said was, "We were worried about you." Dick grinned and replied, "I was just drawn in." We all knew what he meant and that was the end of the matter.

Geoff had a well-honed sense of humour, an encyclopedic knowledge of polar exploration and many good stories. A student on one of his ventures called him "doctor." Geoff snapped back, "This isn't a field hospital." At times, he seemed to be focusing his eyes on some distant horizon and the lands beyond it. On the ice, he sucked his pipe, shared all duties in the tents, and kept up our morale with his tales. He knew Constance Conybeare, widow of Sub-Lieutenant (later Rear Admiral) Crawford James Markland Conybeare, the youngest officer on the Nares Expedition of 1875-76. She confided to him, "Crawford was awfully fond of water for sailing on and bathing in, but *not* for drinking."

Geoff had no talent for self-promotion like so many polar travellers these days. He said: "I tended to regard northern Ellesmere

Island just as a place whither one went in summer, rather than sit at a desk, like most people."

He told us of meeting Odaq, the last survivor of Peary's North Pole party, in 1954, the year before the Inuk died. In 1954 Geoff took two Inughuit with him to the north coast of Ellesmere Island. After a while, they became quite unhappy at being away from home, so Geoff let them leave, after picking up a few tips on how to drive the dogs they left behind. We often discussed polar explorers; Geoff never criticized them. Those who have never experienced travel in the hard places of the world know little of what it involves, so you get silly debates about such matters as the Peary-Cook controversy. Neither reached the North Pole, but both men are worthy of respect. Peter Freuchen said the last word on these two very different explorers: "Cook was a liar and a gentleman. Peary was neither." With his passion for finding cairns, Geoff retrieved some of the messages left by those who had preceded us on Ellesmere Island. In 1953, he found one left by Conybeare near Alert; it contained a jar of excellent navy rum.

Like Harwood, Geoff had a picturesque turn of phrase, referring to hip-waders as "Jesus Boots" – for walking on the water. He gave a hilarious imitation of the wife of the Governor General of the Falkland Islands and described a dull slide presentation he attended: "It went on and on. Finally, someone slipped a slide of the king into the projector. Everyone stood up, sang the National Anthem – and left."

Like a true leader, Geoff made no demands on us that he could not himself meet.

A Congenial Lot

In *North of Latitude Eighty*, his account of Operations Hazen and Tanquary, Geoff noted, "As field leader of the [Lake Hazen] operation, I could not have wished for better balanced or more congenial teams during the two summers."

I came to know some of my companions on the expedition very well, but have only vague recollections of some of the others. I saw Jim Soper and John Tener while we waited for transportation south in Thule in August 1958, but had no other contact with them. I shared a tent with Keith Arnold in 1957, with Brian Sagar in 1958 and with Geoff in 1960.

One example shows the kind of fellowship and dedication that emerged on Operation Hazen. In June 1957, John Filo and Hal Sandstrom arrived to help Fraser Grant with seismic work on the glacier. Two weeks later I emerged from my tent to see a figure struggling up the glacier.

Who could this be?

I jumped on a snow toboggan and set out to meet our visitor. Several kilometres down-glacier, I encountered a figure I did not recognize. Grey-bearded, gaunt, bronzed, shirt flapping under his parka, soaked to the skin, Roger Deane looked like an Old Testament prophet in the wilderness. At forty-eight he was the oldest member of the expedition.

What had impelled him to walk from the lake camp to the glacier just as the melt season began and the rivers were in spate? We hurried Roger back to our tents where he stripped off his wet clothes and slipped into my sleeping bag. Before he fell asleep he told us of the reason for his seventeen-hour journey. While sorting out supplies and equipment that arrived on the plane that brought in Hal and John, he put aside a box marked "Tractor Parts." On opening it later, he discovered it had been mislabelled. The box contained a solarimeter, a device for measuring solar radiation, a vital factor in determining whether the glacier was melting and by how much. Realizing how important this instrument was, Roger set out for the glacier camp, pushing through ice water up his chest at times.

I examined the solarimeter; it had to be plugged into an electrical outlet to operate. Roger's arduous journey had been for nothing. It exemplified the spirit of Operation Hazen – the willingness to help others and to contribute to the success of the venture, no matter what the hardships were.

Roger, nicknamed "Foxy" by his friends, had the reputation as a bon vivant. On our journeys to and from Ellesmere Island, we became incredibly scruffy. Roger always looked as if he had just stepped out of his office at the University of Toronto. At an age when most geologists give up fieldwork, he developed an interest in limnology, the study of lakes. Roger radiated cheerfulness, even after his ordeal. He spent a few days with us, and then we took him down the glacier – with the solarimeter – as far as we could on the snow toboggan and he headed back to the base camp.

In 1958, Operation Hazen had a member who provided equal amounts of frustration and amusement. Like Orde Lees on Shackleton's *Endurance* expedition, he became the odd man out. Mike, as he became known, could easily have become a scapegoat and the butt of our frustrations. Instead he provided comic relief and his sense of humour eased his path to acceptance among us. Anyone coming to the glacier from the base camp brought up special treats – fresh bread, char – for us. When Mike arrived his backpack contained only a selection of cheeses and tins of anchovies for his personal use. A geographer of French extraction, Mike continually spoke about "my most important work."

We never did find out what this was. Someone at the base camp remarked that Mike's method of work amazed everyone. He never spent more than three hours a day on it, and seemed to be making up what he did as he went along. After a few days on the glacier, he grabbed an ice chisel and began to hack at the surface, which was pitted with cryaconites, small deposits of dirt and algae that had sunk into the ice. "We must determine if they are connected," Mike announced before giving up on this piece of scientific research.

We concluded that the reason he joined Operation Hazen was because his boss wanted him out of the office during the summer. Mike spent a lot of time in the tents and the base hut or just standing around on the glacier. We had plenty of work, but he never offered to help. A seismic party going up glacier invited him to join them, believing he would be useful. This did not prove to be the case, so they asked Mike to make the midday meal. We cooked on Coleman stoves which had one problem. When you primed them, some of the fuel dripped out and pooled at the bottom of the stove. As you lit the burners, the whole stove went up in flames. Grabbing a glove, you hurled it out onto the ice. Retrieving it when the fire had gone out, you then tried again to light the stove. Mike entered the tent to start the meal. Suddenly a great sheet of flame burst from the tent door. The other members of the party waited to see the Coleman stove fly out of the door. Instead, a panic-stricken Mike emerged and someone else had to enter the tent and throw out the blazing stove.

Our visitor, bent on showing his intellectual superiority, graded everyone on their ability to speak French. An ardent French nationalist, he never tired of talking of *la grandeur de la France*, the superiority of European culture and the inferiority of the North American way of life. Mike claimed that I had "a Catholic spirit and a French-Italian temperament." I did not know whether to feel insulted or flattered. He spent a lot of time in the tent that I shared with Brian Sagar. Our talk improved my French, while Brian sat reading, breaking off once in a while to make a remark he knew would rile Mike. One was, "All the Catholic Church has done is to make superstition respectable." On another occasion, he remarked, "There are two schools of thought in the world today. One says, 'Bomb the Kremlin,' the other 'Bomb the Vatican.' I'm a member of both schools." Mike would sigh and say, "Ah, Brian. *Vous êtes un libre penseur*."

We all became quite fond of Mike, who headed back to the base camp when he had eaten all his cheeses and anchovies.

At the end of the season, Geoff asked several of us, including me, to stay behind to tidy up and secure the camp. The others flew by helicopter to the US Coast Guard cutter *Atka*, which would take them to Thule. Jim Croal, our liaison officer with the Americans, made it his first priority to evacuate Mike. Geoff had become very short with Mike as he insisted on staying at the base camp to do his "most important work." Jim said, "You get on board that ship or SHIT." Thoroughly scared, Mike bleated to Roger, "The commander said to me SHIT." In his calm way, Roger replied, "Well, if he said that, he probably meant it." Mike jumped aboard the chopper.

The Reason Why

I joined Operation Hazen because Svenn Orvig asked me and I did not have a job. Brought up with tales of adventure and exploration, I felt flattered by the invitation. The reasons others joined the expedition fell into two categories – the urge for adventure and the desire for professional advancement. The two categories are not mutually exclusive.

As Dingle Smith, a member of the winter party, put it: "In [Britain] research was a bit like crossing *t*'s and dotting *i*'s." Ian Jackson, another winterer, summarized his motives for volunteering as twenty percent *la gloire* and eighty percent practical, adding, "It's what the British do. I grew up reading about Scott and Shackleton, and there was a chance to gather material for my PhD dissertation." Ian noted that both he and Dingle were born under the sign of Aquarius, "demonstrating an inquisitive, exploring attitude to life, but may be lacking in imagination and an instinct for disaster." Ian and fellow winterer John Powell were also recruited by Svenn Orvig. They had spent a year as graduate students at McGill and shared an apartment.

Dingle Smith was an unknown quantity as far as the others were concerned. A close friend of Ian's at the University of London, he had doubts about spending a winter in the High Arctic. Hailing from Palmers Green in North London, he had never lived away from home. As he explained, "As a lad, I devoured polar literature and I was a very keen boy scout. They were key motivations. More minor ones were that I would be paid reasonably well and [my involvement with Hazen] could lead to a master's degree at McGill, which had an excellent reputation."

John Powell had also been raised, "some might say brainwashed, on Scott and Shackleton" and had no doubts that "polar exploration was an opportunity to be seized if it presented itself." Dick Harington, a Canadian chosen as leader of the winter party, went to the Arctic "because it was there," as he put it, adding that his father had served for many years in the north with the RCMP "and his stories stimulated me."

Nothing these four men had read prepared them for what happened during the winter of 1957-58 on Lake Hazen. The hut at the base camp had a plywood door and they had problems with the stove, heater and radio, yet they kept up a full schedule of weather observations in the deep cold of the Lake Hazen basin.

Ian described Dick as being *prima inter pares* – first among equals. John noted that if an argument broke out that divided the party, one of them always moved to the other side to restore harmony. Their experiences in extreme isolation, cut off from the outside world save for a few airdrops, offer valuable insights into how people undergoing space travel can adapt to cramped quarters and extended periods in close contact with other humans. A publisher rejected Ian's manuscript on the party's experiences as being "too cheerful." Arctic living is supposed to be about hardships, struggle and suffering.

In contrast to the four winterers, our archeologist, Moreau "Max" Maxwell, had an adventurous life before joining Operation Hazen. A US Navy dive bomber pilot in the Pacific theatre during the Second World War, Moreau later travelled in Burma, Thailand, Vietnam and Cambodia, and then worked on the DEW Line and sledged along the seventieth parallel with Inuit guides, assessing potential landing sites in the Arctic. Cool, amiable and friendly, Max, as we called him, spent extended periods during the summer of 1958 in the field on his own at old Inuit sites. Jim Soper, the botanist, had no Arctic experience and learned about Operation Hazen from Roger, his colleague at the University of Toronto. Ian McLaren, an aquatic biologist, joined the expedition at the request of his employer, the Fisheries Research Board of Canada's Arctic Unit. Ian had spent six seasons in the Arctic, studying seals and plankton. Of his time with Operation Hazen he reported that he enjoyed "the amicable and varied relationships among the disparate members at the base camp. They really were a cultivated lot and I learned much about Arctic botany and geomorphology . . . without any formal background."

John Tener, the mammologist, defined himself as "an adventurer at heart. I always want to see what is over the horizon." He spent five months at Eureka on the Fosheim Peninsula in eastern Ellesmere Island studying muskoxen for the Canadian Wildlife Service. This experience whetted John's appetite for more "High Arctic landscape." John had previously operated on his own or with an assistant. Operation Hazen provided his first experience of working as a member of a team. "The collegial atmosphere at meal times and on many occasions greatly expanded my understanding of other disciplines and generated great respect for those engaged in them."

Bob Christie, the geologist, had about him the look of a small, shy boy. He reacted to every situation by saying, "Gee whiz!" Flying up to Ellesmere Island, Bob seemed to spend all his time filling out official forms with a worried look on his face. He was a very tough traveller, never deterred by distance as he walked over large parts of Ellesmere Island and produced some of the first detailed maps of its geology. He had a sense of dogged persistence about him and a cheerful grin. In 1958 Barry Walker served as his assistant.

My companions on the glacier worked well together.

Keith Arnold, with whom I tented in 1957, came from Cornwall. He had a heart-shaped pixie face and large ears, which he claimed had been pulled into their present shape by a geography teacher seeking to attract his attention. Keith served with the British North Greenland Expedition in 1953-54 after climbing moun-

Bob Christie

tains in Norway, where he met his wife Gunvor. He was the surveyor on the expedition, climbing mountains and locating the bamboo poles erected across the glacier surface that would mark its progress in future years. We had both been in the military, so were accustomed to sharing sleeping quarters. At times, Keith appeared torpid, at other times over-exuberant, testing my patience when he did not do his share of the cooking. Later, he told me that he suffered from bipolar mental illness, passed down from his father. This condition did not affect the quality of his work on the expedition or his ability to travel and climb mountains.

Hans Weber came from Switzerland and proved a continual delight; he said he would have paid to go with Operation Hazen. Geoff asked Hans to be chief geophysicist while he was studying at the University of Alberta. He had served with the Arctic Institute's Second Baffin Island Expedition in 1953. Hans loved challenges and, with his Swiss colleagues, climbed Mount Asgaard, a 914 metre-high granite tower, considered one of the world's ten most challenging peaks. While ski-mountaineering in 1953, Hans met Meg, an English physiotherapist who shared his enthusiasm for the outdoors, and married her in the following year.

Geoff wanted Hans with him in 1957. In October, 1956, he entered hospital with a neurological condition. At the time, he and Meg were living on a small student fellowship. The doctors could not diagnose his condition, calling it polio so the couple could receive financial support from the government. Jim Croal arrived with a case or two of meat bars, a staple of the expedition, and this kept Hans and Meg going. By early 1958, Hans had recovered enough to be able to ski and joined the glacier party. Resolutely cheerful, he would set off, lurching slightly, with an instrument for measuring gravity on his back.

Fraser Grant took charge of the seismic work, seeking to determine the depth of the glacier. He belonged to the Toronto aristocracy. Two friends stayed at a guest house on the family estate, describing the main house as looking like "a grand hotel." Fraser had the mien of a medieval monk and a quiet sense of humour. Tall and handsome, he went about his work with great intensity. Hal Sandstrom, one of his assistants, came from Estonia. Quiet, amiable, hardworking, he tended to say little during our evening talks in the tent. His companion, John Filo, a rather exuberant person, served only during the summer of 1957.

In the summer of 1958 Brian Sagar became my tent mate. Geoff asked me to find an assistant glaciologist after our first summer on the ice. I met Brian in 1952 when we both worked for the United

Africa Company. He spent his time travelling in the bush, supervising small trading posts. One of my jobs involved taking cash up the line from Kano to Nguru in northeast Nigeria. The company bought peanuts from Lebanese and Syrian middlemen who acquired them from African farmers. They insisted, wisely, that they be paid in hard cash, shillings, rather than in paper money that would be eaten by ants. From time to time, when the train stopped at a remote spot to unload boxes of shillings, I'd meet Brian. We'd chat, then I'd jump on the train while Brian in his truck vanished into the distance in a haze of dust. When he came to Kano we had good times together, selling tickets at the race track and drinking far too much. Brian quit the company in 1955, returning to England to teach geography and chemistry at Manchester Grammar School. We arranged to meet at a pub when I went back to England in the winter of 1957. We sat and chatted in the warm glow of the bar, relishing our renewed contact on a dark and dreary night. We drank Guinness and whisky, and through bleary eyes and cigarette smoke I noticed a dog carrying a glass back to the bar in its mouth.

A thought struck me.

"How are you with dogs?" I asked Brian.

"Not bad," he replied.

"How would you like to go on an Arctic expedition?"

"I'd think about it."

The next time I saw Brian's broad grin was in Churchill in the spring of 1958. He and Geoff hit it off immediately, and together they travelled extensively around the ice cap. Both ran out of tobacco one day and tried to smoke dried tea in their pipes. "How was it?" I asked Brian. "Terrible," he replied.

Brian Sagar

Brian had a laconic sense of humour and a great love of the novels of Dostoyevsky, which he read in the tent on idle days. The excellent chemistry among expedition members, which would today be referred to as "male bonding," made the summers on the glacier a delight. Of course, we all became fed up from time to time, complained about the weather and tired of the monotonous diet. There is, of course, no place to go in the evenings. For all the hardships - they rather resembled uncomfortable periods, as when we awoke during the melt season and found our sheepskins soaked with water – morale remained high. We worked as individuals and as members of teams, doing the dull, monotonous work that forms the basis of all good scientific research. We never saw ourselves as protecting Canada's sovereignty in the Arctic or conquering nature. We felt privileged to have this time in our lives in a beautiful unknown land that would remain inviolate through the centuries.

The Happy Airmen

In 2005, the media featured coverage of the controversy over the ownership of Hans Island in the Nares Strait between Ellesmere Island and Greenland, a chunk of barren, worthless rock claimed by Canada and Denmark. The map of northern Ellesmere Island issued in 1973 by the Surveys and Mapping Branch of the Department of Energy, Mines and Resources shows the island as two semi-circles and gives its ownership as "Canada."

The dispute over this piece of Arctic real estate recalls the claim by Jorge Luis Borges that the 1982 war between Britain and Argentina over the Falkland Islands resembled two bald men fighting over a comb. Vague claims are made by academics that Hans Island will be important when the Arctic melts through global warming and its rich resources in fisheries and mineral wealth will become available for exploitation. Canadians have a persistent belief in the myth of the rich north, seeing it as a cornucopia of resources that can be easily tapped and used for the national benefit. This myth dates back to the days of the Klondike Gold Rush: in the 1960s, an old-timer in Dawson told me that "there's more gold in the hills than ever was taken out of the creeks."

There may be untold wealth in the Arctic – but what is the economic, environmental and human cost of exploiting it? As those who have ventured there well know, this is an unbelievably hostile place for most of the year. The Lake Hazen basin, with its balmy summer, is an exception to the barren and lifeless land that is the High Arctic.

You will find no official records of one of the most interesting exercises in extending Canadian sovereignty over Ellesmere Island. Operation Hazen had superb support from the Royal Canadian Air Force, the Canadian Army and the United States Coast Guard.

In 1957, the RCAF flew us to Lake Hazen from Churchill, Manitoba, brought in our supplies and equipment, took us to the glacier, did an airdrop then departed. In 1958, the RCAF put a ski-wheel DC-3 at our disposal. It greatly extended the scope of the field work, flying parties on and off glaciers and to various places all over northern Ellesmere Island. This was the first time a Dakota had been used at such high altitudes and at such high latitudes. A sign board at the Lake Hazen camp described it as forming "Canada's (Unofficial) Arctic Air Command. *Semper Erectus* (Always Upstanding)."

Under the command of Flight Lieutenant Merv Utas, who completed thirty-seven missions as a bomber pilot during the Second World War before he was twenty, this happy band of airmen saved us a great deal of hard travel and hugely expanded the scope of our scientific research. A sense of mutual respect soon developed between us. We admired them and they admired us, although some of them must have thought we were crazy to spend our summers as we did.

Merv and his crew established an unofficial Arctic Air Command with the penis bone of a walrus as its official insignia. True to Canada's bilingual nature, its sign carried the Inuktitut translation of its Latin motto. Jim Croal assured Merv that *Ooshoo Kokoni* was authentic, but Merv recalls the translation as being "rude, or crude, or maybe both."

The Defence Research Board asked the Royal Canadian Air Force's Air Traffic Command for a ski-wheel DC-3 to provide support for our research in 1958. ATC could not meet this request, but Air Defence Command, another part of the RCAF, located such a plane at its base at Sea Island near Vancouver, where Merv was stationed. As he put it, "We had a much greater need on the BC coast for flying boats or float planes than we did for ski planes."

Flight Lieutenant Merv Utas of the Royal Canadian Air Force

The skis for the DC-3, stored at the back of a hangar, had not been installed on the plane. Only Merv had piloted a ski-wheel plane, and that had been eight years earlier, in Winnipeg. This fact his superior officers "were quite prepared to ignore."

The high cost of operating in the Arctic, and the way in which one small error can have large implications, emerged when the DC-3 developed a problem shortly after arriving at Lake Hazen. A seal between the electrical generator and the engine failed, leading to a serious oil leak. "We had boxes of spare parts, but, as usual in such matters, the thing we needed most was not there," said Merv. He radioed Ottawa and learned that it would take five or six days to send up the part. One day, a C-119 landed on the lake. The pilot, a friend of Merv's, reached into his pocket and handed him an envelope. It contained two seals, one for immediate use and a spare. Merv often wondered what the cost per pound of flying that envelope to us was. A Flying Boxcar on a scheduled flight had been diverted to Lake Hazen, yet another example of the splendid support from the RCAF.

In true Canadian fashion, one of the first things Merv and his crew did was to create a curling rink and organize a bonspiel. Clearing a patch of ice on the lake, they painted circles at each end with glacier dye. Six five-gallon gas cans, filled with frozen water, served as curling rocks. For the match between the aircrew and the scientists, Merv put up the DC-3 as a prize: "To my chagrin, we lost our aeroplane, but fortunately, since no one on the opposing team could operate it, they had to give it back."

These kind of wacky goings-on contribute greatly to polar expeditions and ensure that everyone does not become too serious about what they are doing. When the DC-3 first landed on the Gilman Glacier, one of the crew began to lay out a golf course. Pointing to Mount Nukap, he said, "That will be the first tee." Merv landed the plane near Ward Hunt Island and the crew retrieved a cask of pure alcohol left there by Peary in 1906. Mixed with various ingredients, it became a potent drink known as "Peary's Peril."

Merv and his crew coupled their lighthearted approach to life in the Arctic with serious professionalism and what Merv called "interesting experiences." The DC-3 had to be landed facing up-glacier because "it is very difficult to judge your altitude and landing point when the terrain is falling away beneath you." Landing up-glacier presented a problem because takeoff had to be done down-glacier; the plane had to be turned around one hundred and eighty degrees after setting down on the ice. This involved a tricky maneuver: "If we let the aeroplane come to a full stop, we were not certain that we would have enough power to overcome the drag of the snow and the upgrade to move it. So, on every landing, there was a 'moment of truth.' During our landing run, we had to choose a point where we figured we still had sufficient momentum to turn the aeroplane 180 degrees to face downhill but not too much momentum to damage the undercarriage during the turn. At 'the moment of truth,' I would yell 'NOW.' My first officer would pull back fully on the control column while I would apply full left rudder and power to the right engine and pray that we would get around and not break anything."

Those who have flown in Dakotas have warm memories of this tough aeroplane that never let you down and took you to places in the Arctic where no one else had gone before. Landing the DC-3 at two thousand metres near Mount Oxford offered another "interesting aspect" of Arctic flying. At these elevations, engine power is reduced because the air is less dense. As Merv explained, "I started a take-off run, and after skiing for about a mile and a half . . . it was obvious we would not get airborne." At forty knots, Merv fired the JATO (Jet-Assisted Take-Off) bottles fastened under the fuselage "and the blast gave us the extra push needed to attain flying speed." The landing near Ward Hunt Island in whiteout conditions proved tricky. With the horizon obliterated, it was difficult to determine the height of the plane above the ice. Merv landed and took off with his usual panache.

Merv landed his plane on a glacier near Tanquary Fiord, now named Air Force Glacier in tribute to the vital role he and his crew played on Operation Hazen.

The RCAF sent a psychiatrist to Lake Hazen to check on Merv and his merry men. As one of them put it, "He said he could no longer do his job properly because he was one of us."

On The Ward Hunt Ice Shelf

There is an ice shelf attached to the north coast of Ellesmere Island. The shelf extends west and east from the entrance to Disraeli Fiord. Ward Hunt Island, which sits in the centre of it, at 83° 06' N, 74° 10' W, gives its name to this huge mass of ice.

The 1959 Ward Hunt Ice Shelf Expedition originated with a backward-looking approach taken by the United States Air Force (USAF) during the Cold War with Russia. In 1945, the Americans stepped up their air war on Japan, sending waves of bombers to burn down its cities. Some of the aircraft, damaged by flak, crashed before reaching their bases. The capture of Iwo Jima in February and March and Okinawa in April formed part of a grand strategy for using them as "stepping stones" to the main islands of Japan. They could also serve as safe landing sites for crippled bombers and save the lives of airmen. The Americans lost 19,341 troops killed and 64,000 wounded taking the two islands; the Japanese dead totalled 131,000.

If the Cold War had turned hot, American B-52 bombers would have flown over the North Pole to attack targets in the Soviet Union. Returning B-52s damaged by enemy action would need safe landing sites. So the United States Air Force undertook studies to locate them in Greenland and Canada's High Arctic. The 1959 expedition to the Ward Hunt Ice Shelf was rationalized as being "for the purposes of geophysical investigation." USAF contracted with the Arctic Institute of North America (AINA) to supply certain personnel.

I was offered the leadership of Canada-US Ellesmere Island Ice Shelf expedition, but turned it down. After writing up my research results from Operation Hazen, I decided to quit the Arctic, find a steady job and live a normal life.

The Montrealer magazine had offered me a job selling advertising. On the Sunday before starting work, I went skiing in the Laurentians with a group of friends. I had never skied before and tumbled down a bunny slope. My ankle felt painful but I paid no attention to it and the next day walked around Montreal trying to sell advertising. Ten days after the accident I visited a girlfriend in hospital. A nurse who had been in the skiing party asked about my ankle. "A trifle painful," I replied. "Better get it X-rayed," she advised. I did so. At eleven that evening I left the hospital in a wheel chair; my ankle was broken.

I phoned the Arctic Institute to determine if the leadership of Ward Hunt Expedition was still available. Someone else had been hired for it, but the USAF needed a glacial meteorologist with High Arctic experience. So I signed on. The expedition would leave from Boston in April and I joined it in February with plenty of time for my ankle to heal before departure. While waiting to go to Boston, I began to read what had been written on northern Ellesmere Island at the Arctic Institute's Montreal office. One day, a beautiful library student, Pat Wicks, came to do her practice there. I took one look at her and was smitten. She would move to Vancouver when she graduated and I would leave in a few weeks time for Ellesmere Island.

I was paid $730 a month on the ice shelf expedition, plus $5 a day in isolation and danger pay. The Defence Research Board gave me $50 to serve as Canadian liaison officer and for this sum I protected the nation's Arctic sovereignty during the summer of 1959.

The money proved to be poor consolation for participation in an Arctic undertaking ill-starred from the very beginning. USAF assigned a C-130, a plane recently brought into service, to take us to the ice shelf. It had other duties so expedition members waited in Boston, where AINA had an office, until it was available.

Here I found a good friend in Paul Walker, the expedition's glaciologist. He had served at the Ellsworth Station on the Filchner Ice Shelf in Antarctica in 1957-58. We had much in common and both of us were in love. We haunted the bookstores, wandered the streets, ate well and talked endlessly of many things. An eerie experience foreshadowed a future event. We saw Jules Dassin's 1956 movie *Celui qui doit mourir* ("He who must die."). While on a canoe trip on the ice shelf, Paul suffered a brain hemorrhage. Paralyzed, he was airlifted from Ward Hunt Island to hospital for an operation. After my return from the ice shelf, I visited him at his parents' home in Pasadena, California. My friend lay in a hospital bed, blind in one eye and paralyzed down his right side. Some of the old spark remained in this tall, affable Californian, but he never recovered and died later. I submitted Paul's name to the Board on Geographical Names; Walker Hill on Ward Hunt Island serves as a reminder of our friendship.

While waiting in Boston, AINA assured us that we would obtain our arctic clothing at Thule. Paul and I dug in our heels and refused to leave until we had our arctic gear. AINA sent us a cheque for $1,000 and with other expedition members we went to a military surplus store to buy back some of the clothing the US Air Force had sold to the dealer.

Frank Crowley, a geophysicist, led the expedition. I liked him but he never had my respect. I lost confidence in Frank even before we left Thule for the ice shelf. Our supplies and equipment had been piled up at the base without regard to what we would need first when we landed on the ice shelf. After the chaos that Geoff encountered at Thule in 1957, he asked me to go to Churchill in the spring of 1958 and ensure that all supplies and equipment were ready and in order for the expedition. At Thule in 1959, we broke open huge crates in search of small, vital items. While we were doing so, a strapping wire wanged back and slashed open the forehead of an expedition member; it took five stitches to close the wound. No one at the air base offered to help us load the plane; Frank shook us awake at four one morning to tell us this. We dressed, secured a truck and drove three kilometres to a hangar, only to find the plane locked and no one around – the C-130 had hydraulic problems and could not fly.

The captain of the C-130, when it became available, did not seem too pleased with the idea of landing his plane on the ice shelf. In 1954 two USAF colonels, who obviously relished the challenge, had flown Geoff and his team to the ice shelf in two Dakotas. Captain Khoury did not know if the much heavier C-130 could land safely on the ice, nor did we. In five trips, the plane brought in seventy tons of food, supplies, equipment and a bulldozer, tractor, a DUKW (an amphibious vehicle), several snowmobiles, and an aluminum trailer that would be parked at the edge of the ice rise and serve as my base for the meteorological program.

The Ward Hunt Ice Shelf and others along this coast originate as tongues from glaciers that move into the frozen ocean from fiords and inlets. An ice rise links the ice shelf to Ward Hunt Island. The ice shelf grows from the bottom up and has an undulating surface of parallel ridges and troughs that fill with water during the melt season. Peary had one of his hardest journeys when he explored this coast in 1906 and returned through a waste of water and ice.

The Ward Hunt Ice Shelf. (RCAF photo)

After the plane left, we built a hut on the island and the tractor towed the trailer six kilometres north of Ward Hunt Island. Here I erected a Stevenson Screen to house the weather instruments and set out gauges and other devices for measuring snowfall and solar radiation.

Frank had been told to look out for Soviet submarines in the Arctic Ocean. From time to time we'd panic him by reporting their presence after scanning the ice with binoculars. Then we'd say, "Sorry, Frank, just another piece of ice, not the conning tower of a Russian sub." In the middle of summer, Frank received a message saying that his father lay dangerously ill. He radioed for a plane and took off, disrupting the research schedule, leaving no directions to his team. By the time Frank reached him, his father was well on the way to recovery.

Because of our late start and his absence, Frank tried to make up for lost time by working long and irregular hours. He had an alarm clock to wake up members of his team. One of them borrowed mine, which did not ring, and substituted it for Frank's so everyone could get more sleep. On one occasion, Frank set out with a companion to cross Disraeli Bay on a snowmobile. The machine had seen hard service and was in poor condition. The temperature hovered around -20°C. To make matters worse, the two men, inadequately clad, took only half a sleeping bag with them "and not enough food to feed a pigeon," in the words of Staff Sergeant John Grady. Described as a "journeyman" on official documents, John looked after our radio and vehicles. He had been on another venture with Frank in Alaska. On that, Frank took apart a $25,000 instrument because it was not working. "Throwing two switches was all that was needed," John told us.

On Operation Hazen, Geoff never gave the impression of worrying and his sense of confidence infused the enterprise. We knew that he was looking out for us and would not put us in harm's way. On the ice shelf Frank worried perpetually while seeming at a loss about what to do about problems. Tom Turnbull, an army private, and my assistant on the meteorological program, and I lived mainly on C- and K-rations that may well have been left over from the Second World War. We sorted through the cases for the more edible items, discarding the rest. A large pile of cartons containing what we considered to be inedible rations piled up outside the trailer. Frank took it at the end of the season to continue the seismic work. He threw into it all the food we had discarded to sustain himself and his team.

An MIT professor supplied a wide range of materials to be laid on the ice to determine if they could be the basis of a landing strip. We laid out squares of plastic, metal and other material on the ice rise. When the melt came they either sank into the ice or floated away.

The amphibious DUKW – another piece of Army surplus – proved to be a mixed blessing. It worked well before the melt season, then bogged down in pools of slush between the ridges on the ice shelf. It took herculean efforts to move the vehicle on to solid ice. On one occasion, the DUKW slid sideways into a melt pool, filled with slush and almost sank. Frank and the seismic team would take the machine to the edge of the ice shelf. Here it would throw a track that had to be replaced. Frank and his companions would trudge back to Ward Hunt Island, radio Thule and the air force would send a plane to drop a new track near the DUKW. These had to be acquired from a company in California which made them by hand.

The weather did not help my mood.

Storms moved in from the Arctic Ocean and strong winds rocked the trailer. During calm periods, fog bows circled our dwelling. Moving a few metres from the trailer to the instruments on the ice froze me in seconds as I bucked the wind and blowing snow. Occasionally the sun shone and the landscape lifted your heart. The north coast appeared, crystal clear, a magnificent sight. The Challenger Mountains rose up from the ice, and we could see Rambow Hill to the west. Named by the British Arctic Expedition in 1876, it resembled the prow of a battleship of that era.

In 1893, Fridtjof Nansen, from Norway, attempted to drift to the North Pole on the *Fram*. When it became obvious that the ship would not reach the pole, the explorer took Frederick Johansen with him and set off to sledge to it. Blocked by heavy ice and open water, the two men headed for the northern tip of the Franz Josef archipelago. Wintering here, Nansen discovered he'd made a mistake in choosing his companion. Johansen had little to say to him beyond "good morning." Nansen spent a winter without the consolation of good conversation.

I had no say in selecting Tom Turnbull as my assistant. We lived together in the trailer in cramped quarters. Many times during that long summer I had murderous thoughts about Tom as I strove to cope with this cocky mid-westerner. In 1909, Ross Marvin, a thirty-five-year-old university instructor, led one of Peary's support parties to 86° 38' North. On his return, a member of his team, a young Inuk, became exhausted and asked to travel on one of the sledges. Marvin refused to allow this. A cousin of the boy shot the American and pushed his body through a lead in the ice. He reported that Marvin had drowned, only confessing to the murder when he became a Christian in 1924. The man escaped punishment, in part because no one knew in whose jurisdiction the crime had taken place. A peninsula on the north coast and islands at the mouth of Disraeli Bay are named for the unfortunate American.

If I disposed of Turnbull in a similar fashion – we had a rifle in the trailer – I'd have to do all the weather observations round the clock. And Tom rarely left the trailer. We had nothing in common and never bonded. To ease relations between us, I took the twelve-hour "night shift" and Tom did the weather readings during the day. I exploded with anger when I discovered that he had mixed up the readings from two solarimeters. One measured incoming radiation, the other outgoing radiation. The difference between them, given as a percentage, measures the albedo of the ice and snow surface, its degree of reflectivity. The mix-up in the readings made

Jim Lotz, with rifle, and Tom Turnbull at the trailer on the edge of the Ward Hunt Ice Shelf.

meaningless a vital part of the summer research. Added to this aggravation, Tom went through the cartons of C- and K-rations, searching for cigarettes to sell back in the barracks, refusing to share them with other expedition members when they ran out of smokes.

The breakdowns of the DUKWs yielded one benefit – frequent airdrops that included fresh food. I exulted when we received a consignment of lettuce and tomatos. Tom's only comment was, "Uh huh. No salad dressing."

My time with Tom Turnbull made me aware of how personal relationships on polar expeditions can cause endless problems. John Grady showed me how the tensions of isolation can be alleviated through the presence of a joker in the group. John – although apart from his wife, who bore twins while he was on the expedition –

remained cheerful and upbeat throughout our stay. He acted as a minder for Frank, his hard-nosed and realistic attitude to Arctic living contrasting strongly with that of our leader. Collecting kit for the expedition, John fascinated women friends with talk about -85°F weather and the need for "penguin repellant." He had a solemn and serious way of talking nonsense.

Tom collected rocks and wanted to take them back to the States with him. John frowned on learning this: "You can't take rocks across the border." "Why?" asked Tom. "It's because of the lemming die-off. We have to protect the vegetation." Tom accepted this bizarre explanation and left the rocks behind.

You never knew what John would do next. He stapled Frank's mukluks to the floor and attached a smoke grenade to the tool compartment of a snow toboggan. It went off when Dan, our hydrologist, opened it; he was not amused. John tried a similar prank with the toilet paper holder in the latrine. He hoped to catch Frank, warning the rest of us to take toilet paper with us when nature called – and a camera for a photo of Frank enveloped in smoke. This particular trick, however, did not work as Frank found the grenade.

The Americans eventually decided to work with nature on the ice rise, rather than against it. Instead of putting down artificial material on the ice as the basis for a landing strip, the US Navy sent in a team with powerful pumps on the plane that took us out in September. Flooding certain parts of the ice and letting the water freeze would create a suitable surface on which a bomber could land. Frank worried about whether there would be enough available water to do this. One day in late August, John told Frank to stop worrying: "I've found plenty of water." While he was driving the bulldozer, the ice gave way, pitching the machine into a deep pool. We threw a tent over it and installed Coleman stoves to warm us as we jacked up the machine. From time to time a stove went out, spewing raw gas into the confined space. I took breaks in the dull grey world outside the tent, neglecting to wear snow goggles. After two days' hard work, we recovered the bulldozer – and I found I could not open my eyes without extreme pain. The combination of raw gas and ice glare had blinded me; my eyes felt as if they were filled with fine sand. For a day or two I wore two pairs of snow goggles and had to be led to meals and around the Ward Hunt Island camp.

It seemed like a fitting end to a fruitless endeavour that produced nothing of practical value and very little of scientific worth.

By September, all our vehicles lay around the camp, broken and useless. On his 1954 expedition to the ice shelf, Geoff took two Inughuit dog drivers and their sledges with him. The Greenlanders returned home in June, leaving behind fourteen dogs and a sledge with Geoff and his three companions. They did sterling service and were in excellent shape at the end of the season.

We had dogs with us on Operation Hazen, which was probably the last large scientific expedition to use them. In many ways I preferred their company to that of others on the ice shelf – at least the dogs knew how to behave in the Arctic. I learned a great deal about the Arctic – and myself – on the ice shelf. The summer had one major benefit. Had I not broken my ankle and joined the expedition I would never have met Pat. And marrying her made up for any small miseries I suffered in the summer of 1959.

The Americans mounted another expedition to the ice shelf in 1960 on which Brian Sagar served. Soon after this, missiles replaced bombers as the preferred way of sending death over the Arctic. The Ward Hunt ice shelf began to calve in the winter of 1961-62, losing six hundred square kilometres as five ice islands broke away from it. In 1982, another ice island measuring forty kilometres by forty kilometres, sixty metres thick, followed suit; in 1985 Canadian scientists established a base on it as the island drifted southwest off the coast of Axel Heiberg Island. In 2000-2002, the ice shelf along the north coast of Ellesmere Island fractured.

The two expeditions on which I served demonstrate the difference between pure and applied science. The results from Operation Hazen were disseminated widely and sent to the Russians, among others. Those from the ice shelf were classified, and of little use to anyone interested in Arctic research.

Chapter 5

Companions – Canine

Can you remember your huskies all going,
Barking with joy and their brushes in the air?
> – Robert Service, "Men of the High North"

Scott called his dogs "beasts." Amundsen referred to them as "his children." We had mixed feelings about the dogs we hired. On the glacier we tried our hand at driving them but never developed the knack. The dogs soon realized they were with amateurs. Once you hitched a team to a sledge – no easy feat – you pointed it in the direction you wanted to go. Shouting "Mush!" you hoped the dogs would do this. But you never took that for granted.

In 1957, Geoff hired two teams of dogs from Kanaq in Greenland. Half a team stayed at the base camp and the rest joined us on the glacier. The huskies jumped out of the DC-3 on to the glacier surface, scared, snarling, unruly. At first we handled them gingerly, having heard tales of the ferocity of these animals. They all looked alike with their wagging tails, lolling tongues and insatiable appetites. We did not know their Inuktitut names and so were unable to curse them in their native language as we struggled to learn how to make best use of them. Their unique personalities slowly emerged and we gave the dogs individual names.

The full team we had during both summers worked hard. It had a fine *kingmik*. Kippy, "a most gentlemanly dog," as Brian noted, proved very affectionate. At least with humans. As lead dog, Kippy asserted his authority in every way and on every day to keep his team under his control. In camp, the husky made his rounds, beating up each dog in turn to show who was boss. In the traces, he moved to the front of the pack, racing ahead of the others, happy to be doing his job, putting enormous energy into the task of leadership. All the rest of the team took his beatings, literally, lying down. All save Nukap, whom we named for the famous Inughuit traveller. With a fierce glint in his eye, he challenged Kippy, but lost every fight.

One attempt to show leadership almost cost Nukap his life. Geoff, Fraser and Hal went up-glacier on a seismic shoot. The team came to a crevasse in the ice. Standard procedure here is for all the dogs to leap across it at once. Nukap decided to show leadership and leapt across on his own. Falling out of his harness he fell to the floor of the crevasse, howling all the way. Geoff rolled a rope ladder into the crevasse, descended it and watched Nukap as Fraser and Hal hauled him to the surface of the glacier. Apart from a damaged shoulder, the husky appeared unhurt. When the seismic team returned to camp, we decided to give Nukap a holiday. He stayed with me when his team next went up-glacier. Emerging from the tent one day, I saw Rex and another member of his team viciously attacking Nukap. Their teeth were at his throat by the time I separated them. A day or so later, Nukap broke free of

Pack dogs carrying Yvette's puppies in specially made tote-bags.

his trace and headed up-glacier. I chased him for three hundred metres. By the time I stopped, winded, Nukap had not slackened his pace and received a rapturous welcome from his team mates when he rejoined them.

The dogs provided equal amounts of amusement and frustration.

One member of Kippy's team had a most serious mien, and gave the impression of putting all his energy into hauling the sledge; we named him Hinks after the distinguished secretary of the Royal Geographical Society who served from 1915 to 1945. One day, quite suddenly, all the other dogs turned on him. Why was this animal singled out for such savage treatment? Sometimes a sledge dog works too hard – or slacks off – and has to be brought into line. By the time we rescued Hinks, he had been scalped and his coat badly torn. Hinks stayed with me at the glacier camp for a few days, looking like a tonsured monk, while his team worked up-glacier. His eyes shone with gratitude one day as I took the dog his daily feed. As soon as the food hit the ice, a dog from another team jumped him. Hinks survived this attack, and by the end of the season was back in harness with the rest of his team. They may have figured that they had to do more work without him so left Hinks alone.

One dog escaped Kippy's beatings. Hornchurch, an old dog, had a world-weary look to him, giving the impression that he'd been everywhere and done everything a husky could do. With his tacky, tattered coat, Hornchurch little resembled the traditional appearance of an Inuit husky. We surmised that Kippy's kindness to this oldtimer may have been because he was his son. The other dogs tolerated Hornchurch and he may have fathered them all. The husky suffered from a peculiar and painful problem that may have attracted the sympathy of the other animals. He had short legs and a permanent erection. Unable to keep up with the other dogs at times, he would be tossed upside down on the trail. While snow covered the ice of the glacier, Hornchurch had an easy time. When the melt came, and the dogs dashed over the rugged, rough ice surface, the husky's protruding member suffered serious damage. After a day on the trail, the old dog would lie on his side, gazing sadly at his appendage, heaving great sighs of pain and grief. A born slacker, and a greedy animal, he survived the summer in reasonable shape.

The behaviour of the half-team we had with us in 1957 convinced us that they were family pets, not working dogs. Rex, a handsome dog with a red coat, looked strong and noble, like an ideal *king mik*. Thick as two planks, this docile and affectionate husky had no idea about how to lead a team. Another dog we named Englebrecht served as his alter ego, forever leading Rex astray, urging him to break free of his traces. When the people at the base camp sent up a consignment of Arctic char, we ate half of it immediately and put the rest in a store tent; we had no need of a refrigerator. Rex broke loose and scoffed the lot.

Rex had a girlfriend, Yvette, often nuzzling her affectionately. Small and almost completely black, the bitch had soft brown eyes and a gentle demeanour. It soon became apparent that Yvette was in a delicate condition. We released her from sledging duties, a privilege rarely accorded a working husky. She became very affectionate, but refused to be spoiled and gave birth to eight healthy puppies just before we left the glacier.

Two other dogs in Rex's team had distinguishing features. One, a near albino, we called Whitey. Another, whose name I have forgotten, suffered from paranoia, panicking every time anyone came near him. During the melt season, he ran away from me, tripped over his trace and landed in a melt stream. Crafty Englebrecht would chew his traces and escape. To teach him a lesson, we hobbled him, put him in a basket, placed another on top of him and tied them together with a thick rope. Somehow, Englebrecht escaped. We thought of renaming him Houdini.

Kippy's team moved with grace and speed over the glacier in 1957 and 1958. In our second year we used a less satisfactory team. We named its leader Admiral Jim after Jim Croal. It included Rusty, named for the colour of his coat (Keith said he looked like a dishonest bookmaker), Tweedledum and Tweedledee (because we could not tell them apart), Aunt Maud (who looked refined but went crazy from time to time and beat up Rusty), Harwood, Lion (a complete misnomer for a timid creature) and Popsie, a bitch. Droopy Drawers, another member of this team, suffered from acute constipation. To ease his sufferings I once put seven Milk of Magnesia tablets down his throat.

The huskies seemed baffled when first we hitched them to a Nansen sledge, leaping about and tangling their traces. Admiral Jim's miserable bunch often fought with each other, drawing blood. Their behaviour stemmed from the lack of a strong lead dog like Kippy, who ensured that the team worked together efficiently.

We had two types of sledges – Greenland and Nansen. The former came from Kanaq. Geoff had used them on the 1953 and 1954 expeditions and learned how to drive dogs from his Inughuit companions. The Greenland sledges consisted of two wooden run-

Brian Sagar at the camp on the Gilman Glacier in 1958. The pyramid tents are immediately behind him while the Logan tent is in the background to the left. A Nansen sledge is in the foreground.

ners (the Inuit used bone or even frozen salmon in the past) connected by slats. The sledges look ungainly, but they are very flexible and this helps when travelling over rough ice. Nansen sledges have a light framework on two ski-like runners While waiting for the other expedition members in Churchill in 1958, Geoff asked me to assemble a Nansen sledge. He believed I could do this. And much to my surprise, with the help of an article in *The Polar Record* and the staff of the Defence Research Board's Northern Laboratory, I succeeded.

We used the fan trace, also known as the Thule trace, to attach the dogs to the sledges. It allows each dog to pick its own way forward. Crary, a dog named for one of Geoff's companions on the ice shelf in 1954, always wanted to look over the landscape – or rather snowscape – so he moved to the edge of the pack and kept a position there. The long trace, used in forested areas, involves hitching dogs behind each other or in pairs. In this way, they avoid wrapping themselves – and the sledge – around trees. This trace is also used in deep snow in river valleys and fiords. The king dog breaks trail for the others – or a human can walk ahead of the team and make a path for it.

Our first task each morning involved untangling the traces of the dogs. They were attached to ice anchors or secured in other ways; straightening them out could take up to an hour. While Brian did so one day, a dog peed on his leg. He rounded on it and the husky promptly peed on his other leg. Just as you sorted out one trace, the dogs would start fighting and jumping over each other. You had to begin all over again. With all the traces untangled, you then hitched the dogs to the sledge. Geoff had all the traces in his hands one day when the dogs took off down-glacier, dragging him about a kilometre while he split the cold air with choice curses. After Keith hitched up a team, the dogs simply lay in the snow, looking bored, ignoring him. Suddenly they dashed off in all directions while one climbed onto the sledge.

Stopping a sledge presented problems if the dogs had the bit between their teeth and were bounding ahead. The Inuit can stop a sledge with whips and shouts. We lacked their skills. The Greenland sledge can be stopped by throwing a rope over the front of the runners, no easy task when the dogs are going full speed down a glacier. The Nansen has a steel brake at the rear, below the handlebars. The driver steps on it and its point digs into the ice.

We became fond of our dogs and did what we could to keep them in good shape and protect them from some of the discomforts of glacier living. We had volunteered for the expedition; they had been drafted and often gave the impression that they would rather be lazing at home in Kanaq than working for a bunch of intruders. A husky can pull about fifty kilograms, so sledges were loaded with no more than four hundred kilos. Geoff knew exactly how to load a sledge to ensure that everything on it was balanced and nothing fell off. Food boxes went on the bottom slats and the tent on top so that it could be quickly retrieved and erected when making camp.

We all enjoyed sledge travel; travelling by dog team over a glacier on a bright sunny day lifts your spirits and you feel at one with the huskies and the land. We used the dogs extensively before the melt season began. After this we drove them mainly above the firn line where the summer snow had not melted.

Once the melt began, life became very damp and uncomfortable for us and the dogs, which searched for dry places on which to rest. Fraser put down straw and pieces of felt for Rex's team. Yvette immediately lay down on a piece of felt. Laddie could not figure out what to do and simply stared at a patch of straw, thoroughly puzzled. Englebrecht tried to eat the straw. Rex, true to form, broke loose from his trace, headed for the store tent and bedded down on packing material. As small streams coursed through the camp, we set out the baskets used for the airdrop and encouraged the dogs to sit in them. While some of the huskies scorned this comfort, every time Rex returned from a trip, he leapt into his basket and lay there, shivering and bewildered, wondering what cruel fate had spoiled his summer.

The Inuit make sealskin boots for their dogs to protect their feet while travelling over rough ice. In 1958, after seeing their sufferings in the previous summer, we fitted the dogs with rubber boots. They took an instant dislike to them. Kippy in particular looked most undignified. He lifted each leg like a trotting horse, trying to flip the booties off his paws. Obviously, no self-respecting Inuit husky needed such devices to protect itself against ice!

Huskies require lots of calories when pulling loaded sledges. Geoff took horse meat with him in 1953 and 1954 to feed the dogs. The animals needed a great deal of it to sustain themselves so Geoff sought a substitute, a dog food that offered the maximum of nutrition for the minimum amount of weight. He found a product called Nutrican, made by Bob Martin's in England. It came packed in tins holding sixty one-pound blocks, each of which would feed one husky for one day. One tin would sustain a ten-dog team for six days and fitted easily on a sledge. At first, the dogs sniffed at the one-pound blocks and ignored them. When wet, the dog food smelled like old socks left lying around too long. However, in time, the huskies began to relish it and the Nutrican kept them in excellent condition throughout the summer. The local wolves also liked it. We came across a cached can they'd ripped open and emptied.

Hornchurch, a hungry creature, loved this new food and tried to steal blocks we threw to other dogs. On Keith's birthday, we decided to see how much Nutrican the old dog could eat. The husky wolfed down the first three blocks, slowed down after the next three and gave up half-way through the seventh. Hornchurch then lay down and made us regret our generosity by howling for two hours. Having to hunt seal to feed their dogs slowed down Mounties who set out on patrol from small Arctic settlements. On our way south in 1957, we gave some tins of Nutrican to the Mounties at Alexandra Fiord; with it they could travel for days without worrying about finding seals or other food for their dogs.

In addition to dogs, we had two Eliason snow toboggans, an early version of the snowmobile. Manufactured by the Four

An Eliason snowmobile or "motor-toboggan" tows a Nansen sledge (left) on the Glman Glacier.

Wheel Drive Auto Company in Kitchener, Ontario, in 1943, these very basic machines gave us excellent service. You needed no special mechanical knowledge to operate and care for them and they worked equally well in deep, soft snow and on hard pack. Hard pack gave the best "bite" for the toboggan tracks and you could reach speeds of thirty-five kilometres an hour at times. Travel on bare ice strained the frames, tracks and axles.

During the melt season, we used the machines mainly above the firn line. Below it, the snow toboggans sometimes slipped into holes of slush and soft snow and had to be physically heaved onto a firm surface. Two members of a field party made two traverses of the ice cap totalling three hundred and fifty kilometres and only had to walk twenty kilometres when the snow toboggans hit soft snow. The machines weighed only two hundred and nine kilograms and could be easily manhandled; we loaded them in and out of DC-3s without difficulty. They could haul seven hundred kilograms – about twice what we usually put on a sledge hauled by a team of ten huskies.

You can drive a snow toboggan continuously; dogs must be rested regularly. Huskies, with their paws on the ice, cope easily with problems that can cause difficulties for snow machines in whiteout conditions. During a whiteout, land and sky merge into total uniformity and you lose your sense of direction and any feel for the terrain if you are driving a snowmobile. In 1959 I became airborne on a snow toboggan in a whiteout as it soared off a ridge on the ice shelf. These machines cannot operate effectively in rocky valleys or on melting glaciers where dogs travel with ease.

I spent many days alone at the glacier camp, with only the dogs for company. To see the huskies frolicking in the snow, playing with each other, while Hornchurch snoozed in the sun, made me wonder why anyone could complain about living a dog's life. When we used mechanical transport, the dogs jumped on the sledges they towed, quite content to let the machines do the work. True northerners, they knew all about the need to conserve energy in a cold climate.

We lost only one dog during the two summers when its cut leg became gangrenous. Despite the best efforts of the doctor on the US Coast Guard cutter *Eastwind*, which took us to Thule in 1957, the husky had to be put down.

Hans Weber recalled an interesting trip with Kippy's team in 1958. The DC-3 piloted by Merv took him, Keith and Hal to the head of Clements Markham Inlet to measure changes in gravity from tidewater there. The glacier of the same name drains from the central ice cap. The party crossed the United States Range to the Gilman Glacier. From here it continued on to the Lake Hazen basin to reach tidewater at the head of Chandler Fiord. This first crossing of Ellesmere Island at this latitude involved a great deal of hard travel using dog teams and a snowmobile.

After two weeks on the trail, the team came to the glacier camp to exchange Kippy's tired team for a fresh one. When Hans and the others hitched up the new team to a sledge, a terrific fight broke out. Brian and I had named one of the dogs Mark but it was a bitch and in heat. Hans renamed her Marcia and hitched the husky to the sledge towed by the Eliason. Then he opened the throttle. The snow toboggan moved just slightly faster than the dog team behind it. As Hans put it, "For the next three days, until the dogs lost interest in Marcia, we must have had the fastest dog team in the Arctic."

On their way down the Gilman Glacier, the team found itself on the wrong side of a large melt stream. They headed back up-glacier to find an easier place to cross. The dogs decided to return to camp, which they associated with rest and food. Off they dashed, stopping only to pee at bamboo poles set up to measure the melt and movement of the glacier. Dingle Smith observed, "So much for scientific accuracy."

On a dull, dreary day towards the end of the 1957 season, Geoff, Fraser Grant and I went down the Gilman to do a seismic shoot to determine its depth. Thick and clammy fog enveloped us as we finished our work and headed back to camp. While Geoff drove the dogs, Fraser ran alongside the sledge and I sat on it, serving as ballast. Led by Kippy, the dogs pulled the Greenland sledge over the rough ice and we made good progress. At one point, the sledge tipped over, dumping me into a melt pool. Soaking wet, I clambered back on board as Geoff urged on the dogs. We all wanted to reach the warmth of the tent and had not eaten for hours as we completed this last piece of research. Kippy showed his usual dogged determination as we moved through the fog. Geoff's long whip snaked over the dogs as he sought to direct the *kingmik* towards the camp. Kippy resolutely followed his own course, despite Geoff's efforts to move him in another direction; nothing diverted him.

Suddenly, the fog lifted. We saw the camp. The meteorological mast was directly in line with Kippy's nose.

On his trip to the South Pole, Amundsen took a difficult route to the Antarctic Plateau, forcing his dogs up a glacier. They continually sought another path than the one chosen by Amundsen. When he looked back at the head of the glacier, he realized that his dogs had a better sense of direction than he had. The route they had tried to take would have been much easier than the one he chose.

We took dogs on overland trips. In 1957 we made packs from geological sample bags using neck bands to secure them to the dogs. Each dog could carry about eight kilos of equipment or other cargo. In 1958 we had tailor-made dog packs. Bob Christie and Barry Walker made an epic geological traverse from the east end of Lake Hazen to Alert and back, a distance of about two hundred and sixty kilometres. The dogs carried backpacks that enabled the two travellers to take more stuff with them than they could carry on their own backs. The dogs and the humans both suffered much from insects; the animals rolled in mud and water to rid themselves of these pests, an option not available to Bob and Barry.

At summer's end in 1957 we had a hard journey over rough ice to a place where we could walk off the Gilman. I wore a pair of new boots that I had not broken in; they proceeded to break

Barry Walker and three dogs on the Arctic tundra northeast of Lake Hazen. With their tailor-made backpacks, each dog could carry about eight kilograms.

The dogs bedeviled by insects.

me in as I walked over rough and uneven terrain. You could never be sure when you stepped forward whether your foot would hit solid ground, slip off a clump of vegetation or sink into a soggy patch of mud. The dogs trotted alongside carrying packs. Keith had emblazoned titles on them. Droopy Drawers worked for the Kanaq Karrier Company while Hinks had been designated The Hazen Express. Yvette's eight puppies looked snug and safe, sewn into packs on two dogs.

At the snout of the glacier we crossed a melt stream. The dogs swam across the turbulent, ice-cold water as we waded across, soaked to the crotch and feeling numb in our nether parts. We carried our packs and those of the dogs. Yvette kept an anxious eye on her offspring as we held them above the water. She stayed at the far side of the melt stream. Racing up and down the stream bank, sliding into the water and climbing out, this sopping bundle of misery refused to cross the stream. Geoff grabbed a puppy, plunged into the icy water, lured Yvette to him by dangling the puppy at her, caught the husky and carried her bodily across the stream. Reunited with her new family, Yvette looked happy again.

We trudged down the valley of the Gilman River, wet and cold, looking forward to making camp, relaxing and eating hot food. We noted that Nukap had lost his puppy pack and set off up-valley to find it. After an hour's search we heard pitiful bleatings in the wilderness. The lost puppies lay helpless on the ground. Why Yvette had not missed them and gone back to search for them mystified us. Had a wolf found these small dogs before we did, it would have been introduced to the delights of prepackaged food.

The dogs kept pace with us. Every so often we sighted one of the many wonders of Ellesmere Island – enormous gatherings of Arctic hares which carpeted the tundra in white. Off went the dogs in pursuit, their packs bouncing on their backs. The hares stood on their hind legs and ran away at great speed, well ahead of the dogs who soon gave up the chase. True to form, Hornchurch dashed off with the rest of the dogs, ran about fifty metres then lay down, sighing, utterly exhausted.

Kippy carried about sixteen kilos on the walk to the lake. At the end of a long day, this hardworking husky, too tired even to eat his Nutrican, simply lay down and rested. We immortalized our canine companions by naming a stream flowing across Judge Daly Promontory into Archer Fiord after them. Packdog Creek may well be the only Arctic feature paying tribute to these animals rather than to some long-dead Briton or American. We thought Kippy deserved to have a feature named after him, but could not see the Board on Geographical Names accepting it.

We left two puppies with the winter party, who named them Mutt and Jeff after two British cartoon characters. Jeff, the male, did not survive the intense cold at base camp. Mutt, the female, joined us at the glacier camp in the summer of 1958. It became very clear that she had no idea how to behave like a sledge dog. Hitched up with a team, Mutt tried to jump on the sledge. She then put her paws on it and walked alongside "like a bloody kangaroo," as Geoff put it. The winter party presented the dog to the crew of the US Coast Guard cutter *Atka* as a small measure of our appreciation for their evacuation of the expedition members in August 1958. Had Mutt gone to Kanaq she might not have survived since she had lost any inherited ability as a working husky.

In 1957, a Piasecki helicopter flew us from the base camp on Lake Hazen to the US Coast Guard Cutter *Eastwind* at the head of Chandler Fiord. Keith and I, each holding a dog, jumped out of the chopper as it landed on the cutter. The assembled crew members immediately fell back, moving away from us as we struggled to hang on to the dogs. I'm still not sure whether they reacted in

Ancient and modern modes of Arctic travel – husky dogs and a Piasecki helicopter.

this way because they feared the dogs and their alleged ferocity or because we smelled so ripe after three months without washing or bathing.

Within hours, the crew members were spoiling the dogs silly. Rex came into his own in the role of a noble, handsome husky, looking dignified and aloof as sailors admired and petted him. Yvette and her puppies gobbled down candy bars, chewing gum and the best food the ship could offer.

On our way to Thule, the cutter stopped at Kanaq to unload the dogs. A crane slung them over the side, supported by a belly band. In the waiting barge they fought and snarled at each other. Every dog joined in the fray as soon as its paws hit the deck.

Every dog except Hornchurch, that is.

He had fallen overboard. Hauled out of the water, the old dog then went home to his accustomed life.

Chapter 6

Life on the Ice

You looked like fleas on a bedsheet.
— Svenn Orvig's view of the glacier camp from the air

Like the early Inuit, our lives on the glacier revolved around basic concerns. Shelter, food and water, companionship and travel filled our days in a black and white world.

Polar expeditions present a paradox. They attract risk-takers, adventurers, seekers of thrills and new experiences. Yet much of the activity in extreme environments is routine, monotonous, unchallenging. Boredom is a threat and isolation can erode morale. The sheer immensity of your physical surroundings can overwhelm you. Looking back, I recall intense experiences that made me feel fully alive — the hard sledge trips, the perilous walks, the outbursts of extreme weather when I struggled out of the tent or trailer to read instruments. The daily round in the camp left no impressions. I spent as many as nine days on my own on the glacier, yet never felt lonely. Time simply slipped by as I made my routine observations.

On some days, the shining sun made our spirits soar. On others, fog shrouded the camp and seemed to seep into our very souls.

After the blizzard on the glacier subsided, we dug out our supplies and equipment and put the camp in order. During the summer of 1957, two people occupied a pyramid tent with a floor space of 4.6 square metres. In 1958 we had three-person tents for each couple, with 7.5 square metres of space. In that year we put sheepskins over the caribou skins for extra warmth. Unfortunately, they absorbed water during the melt season.

We erected two five-person tents for supplies – they were too big to live in – and a Logan ridgepole tent to serve as my "office." I made a crude desk from a packing crate on which to stand my instruments for recording the weather and with the help of the others raised a ten-metre meteorological mast. On it I installed anemometers to measure wind speed and thermocouples to record temperatures at ten centimetres, one metre, three metres and ten metres above the surface. Leads from the instruments led to the Logan tent where I took the readings. If one of these instruments failed to do its job, I climbed the mast to fix it. Scared stiff, I clung to the flimsy metal structure, sometimes chewing ice off an instrument to make it work. I took readings from them every two hours from eight in the morning until ten in the evening.

My three companions helped me to assemble and erect a Stevenson Screen. Named after the father of novelist Robert Louis Stevenson, it holds automatic, clock-driven devices for measuring weather phenomena – temperature, pressure, etc. It protects the instruments from the weather while allowing air to pass through slats in the boxlike container. Weather readings throughout the world are taken in Stevenson Screens. I read the instruments, which included thermometers that read maximum and minimum temperatures for each day, at 8 a.m., 2 p.m. and 8 p.m. I also mea-

The author up the meteorological mast on the Gilman Glacier. Mount Nukap and Nukap Glacier is in the background.

sured wind speed and direction on the glacier surface, snow and rainfall, sunshine and cloud cover. With other instruments I determined the albedo of the glacier surface, its reflectivity, a vital indicator of how the ice melted through the summer. While I collected data on the weather above the ice surface, Geoff dug into it. We erected a tripod to support an ice corer.

Jim Lotz taking readings in a Stevenson Screen

Observations

In place of the adventurous explorers of [Martin] Frobisher's day, searching for fabled empires and golden cities, there appears in the seas of the north the inquisitive man of science, eagerly examining the phenomenon of sea and sky to add to the stock of human knowledge.

    – Stephen Leacock, *Adventures in the Far North*

Our instruments, by modern standards, were quite simple. And we faced problems in doing our observations. How can you measure falls of snow accurately when the winds blow it horizontally? Or rainfall which barely wets the surface of the container? You record them as "traces," an apt term for the small amounts of precipitation on the glacier. James Thurber wrote about sketching what he saw through a microscope, only to be told by an instructor that he had drawn his own eye. In the same way, I wondered whether my instruments measured the weather on or above the glacier accurately. Or had I created a microclimate around them and was I measuring *that*?

A scientist is only as good as the data she or he collects. Gathering that data depends on instruments that may be faulty. Early in 1999, Environment Canada established the world's most northerly weather station on William's Island, some six kilometres west of Alert. Fully automatic, it runs on batteries during the winter and solar power after the sun rises. Such installations measure weather much more accurately than humans can. An automatic station would not have worked on the glacier as it would have sunk into the ice, tilted over or been washed away in the melt season. Scientists spend a lot of time cursing and fixing their instruments. With our primitive devices, we gathered reasonably accurate data on the weather and other phenomenon in the interior of Ellesmere Island – the first time this had been done. Science involves an endless search for better ways to measure and understand the world. In 1958, with a more sophisticated depth recorder, Roger corrected his earlier estimates of the depth of Lake Hazen.

Geoff extracted cores from the glacier and the ice cap and dug pits to examine the stratified layers of ice in them. We all took turns at hand coring, which makes you feel as if your body has been wrenched out of shape – permanently. This task is now done with the aid of a small motor.

On the Greenland ice cap, huge rigs have drilled cores down to bedrock, three thousand metres below the surface. Glacial ice becomes a time capsule, trapping dust, acid molecules, gasses, volcanic detritus and other airborne bits and pieces through the centuries, recording evidence of atmospheric pollution and climate change from two hundred thousand years ago. The eruption of Mount Tambora in what is now Indonesia in 1815 led to The Year Without a Summer in 1816; it too left traces of ash in glaciers. The cores from Greenland offer evidence of periods of warming and cooling, showing that this happens naturally. The climate of the Eastern and High Arctic has varied over the past years.

The Medieval Warm Period lasted from about 1250 to 1500. The Norse settled in Greenland and the Inuit adapted to changes in wildlife distribution. Then came the Little Ice Age from 1650 to 1850. Ice conditions in Baffin Bay and further north changed greatly, as the history of Arctic exploration reveals. Through ice cores, it's possible to trace the increase in environmental pollution since humans began to put massive amounts of crud into the atmosphere. A core taken from the Agassiz Ice Cap contained traces of a pesticide used only in Texas. How did it reach northern Ellesmere Island?

Geoff's work focused on determining the mass balance of the Gilman Glacier, the amount of snow and ice it had gained or lost over the past few years. We drilled in lines of bamboo stakes across the glacier and Keith located them from nearby peaks. Their position in succeeding years will indicate how fast the Gilman is moving and how much ice it has lost. There are more accurate ways to determine this these days through airborne radar systems and other devices. I took part in several seismic shoots. We exploded charges on the glacier surface. Sound waves from them hit the rock below the glacier ice and bounced back. Geophones on the surface picked up the sound waves. The time it took for the return wave to reach the surface indicated the depth of the ice.

While I remained at the glacier camp, doing a regular round of observations, sledge parties came and went at all hours. Sometimes the others worked fourteen-hour days. Returning cold and wet from their journeys, they rested for a while then loaded up their sledges and headed out again. No one ever complained or showed much concern for their own comfort. We all realized we would be there for a short period and that what we learned would be valuable to others seeking to understand the High Arctic. In 1958, Geoff and Brian travelled across the ice cap to the heads of M'Clintock Inlet, Tanquary Fiord and the Henrietta Nesmith Glacier, sleeping during the day and carrying out glaciological observations during the cold nights when travel was easier.

In the Camp

On the Gilman Glacier we had to solve a number of practical problems. We placed our supplies, equipment and fuel drums in a line in front of the tents. If we had another blizzard they would be easy to find and recover. On the 1959 ice shelf expedition, field parties left tools and equipment on the surface of the ice shelf and returned to the camp on Ward Hunt Island. Sudden snowstorms swept across the shelf, making it difficult to find and recover them.

This rather trivial example points up the nature of scientific problem solving – it merely involves the application of common-sense and reasoning in the search for answers. A problem is external, outside you, solved by applying the best available technology and using the right mental processes. A mystery is internal, inside you. You don't solve mysteries; you explore them. They become more understandable as you enter into a dialogue with the unknown; you change your mental approach as you see deeper and deeper into the mystery.

On the glacier, we recognized that we were simply scraping the surface of a very complex system of natural interactions. We probed the limits of the physical environment, seeking to determine what had happened and was happening on one small part of an immense ice mass. We were also exploring the limits of our own psyches, which were equally immense and almost as little known. We did not have the brash self-confidence of those seeking a better detergent or a more fuel-efficient car. We approached the land and our work with respect and humility, aware of how little we could find in such a short stay in this unknown and unknowable land.

Since I had to stay in the glacier camp, I served as bull cook, keeping the place tidy and in reasonable order. The work filled my hours and met some sort of need related to an impulse to organize things. Personal cleanliness and hygiene consisted of wiping our hands on the caribou skins in the tent and on our clothing, which became stiff with grease and dirt. In truth we lived in a great deal of squalor. Once in a while we heated water and shaved. A beard may fit the image of a polar explorer but it can result in frostbite if it mats and cold freezes the underlying flesh.

At first we wore parkas, windpants, woolen drawers and mukluks with double liners and had trouble telling each other apart. As the weather warmed up, we shed our outer clothing and individual sartorial styles emerged. Geoff favoured a blue wool hat and a bandana around his neck. Keith wore a red Norwegian sweater. This special clothing means a great deal while in isolation for each piece has an emotional connotation, serving as a link to those you left behind and expressing your individualism. My wardrobe consisted of a balaclava (much of the heat of your body leaves through your head, a fact many Canadians appear unaware of in winter), a woolen shirt-jacket, down waistcoat, thick army shirt, woolen drawers and ski pants. On a few occasions on the glacier we stripped to

Getting a suntan on the shores of Lake Hazen

the waist, putting on our shirts at the slightest breeze. At the lake, some of the party sunbathed regularly.

We all smelled rather badly in the pure Arctic air. But since we all smelled the same, no one objected. Women now go north on scientific ventures and I'm sure that living conditions, hygiene, and general cleanliness have much improved. We washed our hands from time to time, but that was as far as personal grooming went.

Geoff issued waders – Jesus boots – when the melt started. Those made of rubber kept our feet dry. The sealskin boots (*kamiks*) proved a bit tight but equally effective. The waders leaked if ice slashed them; we put our soggy socks in the apex of the tent and they soon dried. We carried sheath knives – Geoff kept one in his boot for easy access – and used them for cutting up food, scraping boots, mending instruments and equipment, spearing savoury bits in the cooking pot, and numerous other tasks. Even after the melt began, we never left the tent without snow goggles. The intense direct and indirect solar radiation at this latitude can lead quickly to snow blindness even after the glacier loses its virgin whiteness.

Before I left for Ellesmere Island in 1957, my friend Herman, who worked for CIL, asked me to wear-test a sleeping bag and a parka filled with Terylene. Geoff gave me permission to do this. The sleeping bag and the parka proved serviceable; during July and August I needed only the outer shell of the bag to keep me warm at night. On my return to Montreal I gave Herman a report and some photos. One showed me outside the tent, wearing the parka, with the sleeping bag draped nearby. I held Rex, who looked noble and husky-like. I presented the very image of an Arctic explorer and his faithful hound.

I thought that the report and photos would be filed away in CIL and was surprised to discover that they had given me my fifteen minutes of fame. One of the airdrops in 1958 contained an ad from CIL and an article ("Diamonds in the Snow/*entre ciel et neige*") from the company magazine. CIL ran the photo I gave Herman as part of an advertisement in *Time*, *Hunting and Fishing* and *Forest and Outdoors* – without my permission.

This unwanted publicity had two outcomes. In the base camp I noticed a cartoon pinned on the wall. It showed a husky with two polar types in the background. The dog complains, "We do all the work and they get all the credit." The word "they" had been replaced by "Lotz." On my return south, I spoke to a lawyer friend about the use of the photo and the other material. He told me about unlawful enrichment – a legal concept related to actions from which others derive benefits at your expense. Herman took me to the public relations department at CIL and I secured suitable compensation for my contribution to the promotion of Terylene.

An Arctic explorer and his faithful hound.

Meals

To live in harmony with another person under such stringent conditions demands a certain etiquette – unfailing generosity and politeness.
 – Richard M. Weber and Mikhail Malakhov, *Polar Attack*

The initial phase of a polar expedition sets the stage for what happens in its later course. We had to adapt to living in close quarters very quickly. We crowded into the pyramid tents, finding them cramped and uncomfortable. Irregular, hastily prepared meals gave us all constipation. Our hands became sore from pushing needles through the stubborn nylon of the parachute straps to make dog harnesses. You enter a pyramid tent through a circular opening and cannot stand upright, so in this we resembled the ancient Inuit living in skin tents. Like them, we hung damp clothing from the top of our temporary dwelling. Like the Inuit we made careful use of the small available space. A long wooden box lay between our two sleeping places. The Coleman stove stood on it and the box held food, pots, pans, knives, forks and other utensils. A ration box sat at the rear of the tent. We could make breakfast without leaving our sleeping bags – if the stove behaved.

Trevor Harwood and Geoff put a lot of thought into the food to sustain our bodies and our morale. Food quickly becomes a focus of discontent in isolated places. Stories abound of cooks going berserk when anyone criticizes the meals in camps in the bush. Some chased work crews with cleavers and had to be tied up and shipped out. In the north, poor quality stuff soon decays, rots or disintegrates.

The food on Operation Hazen came in aluminum boxes marked DR (Daily Rations for two people for two weeks) and DS

(Daily Supplementary). You need five thousand to six thousand calories a day to sustain yourself in the Arctic – and variety in what you eat. DR boxes contained basic foods, the DS ones special treats. Each DR box held a can of meat, two kilos of sweet biscuits (never very popular), dates, cocoa, pilot biscuits (in place of bread), six one-pound tins of butter (inevitably consumed in two weeks as the fat kept up our energy levels), egg powder, dried prunes, Marmite (without which no British polar expedition is complete), oatmeal, dried soups, sugar, dried milk (Klim) and chocolate bars.

The DS boxes contained sardines, canned sausages, jam, instant puddings, great rounds of Black Diamond Cheese, orange juice, dried vegetables, curry powder, spaghetti and other delights. A note in each box listed the contents and stated, "Any discrepancies in connection with this delivery should be reported immediately." Each box weighed about thirty kilograms and fitted neatly on a sledge. They withstood a great deal of hard use and when empty served as ideal containers for things such as scientific equipment, spare clothing and tools.

Little thought was given to food on the joint Canada US ice shelf expedition, although we did receive airdrops of fresh fruit and vegetables. But we relied mainly on huge quantities of C- and K-Rations and a few edible items from Filene's store in Boston which soon ran out. We also had Quick Serve Meals put up by the US military – known in the military as "shit on a shingle." They came with detailed instructions for the simple-minded on preparing meals for six men from one package. You had to open the cartons carefully, remove the packages(s) and plastic packs. Dinner No. 2 consisted of chicken and rice soup, spaghetti with meat and tomato sauce, butterscotch pudding, bread, jelly, a chocolate fudge bar and coffee or tea. Alex, the camp manager, tried at first to set meal times and serve the dinners. He soon gave up as people simply rooted in the cartons at any time of day to find items they wanted and prepared them on their own.

Polar narratives contain chilling descriptions of scurvy caused by lack of vitamin C. On Operation Hazen we relied on vitamin pills, ascorbic acid tablets, lime and orange juice to make up for the absence of fresh produce. Our bachelor style of squalid living did not do justice to the food; to us, it was simply fuel to keep us going. We grabbed food and downed it quickly, much as the Inuit did. I expended a lot less energy than those who were always on the trail. A plate of scrambled eggs, a few dates and raisins, tea and orange juice met my nutritional needs when I remained alone in camp.

When everyone was in camp on the glacier, we developed a routine for preparing meals. In the evening we chipped ice, filled a pan and left it outside the tent. In the morning, still in his sleeping bag, the breakfast cook dragged in the pot, sniffed it – in case a dog had broken loose and peed in it – and put some of the ice into another pot, leaving the rest to melt as the tent warmed up. The other man in the tent primed and lit the stove. Sometimes it exploded in flames when a match was applied – a technique known as "pre-heating" – and had to be cooled off by hurling it out of the tent door and then retrieving it. If this did not happen, the melting ice in the pot placed on it served as the basis for morning porridge into which was thrown butter, dates and raisins. Sometimes the stove ran out of fuel with the mush half-cooked. We had then to decide whether to remove the fuel tank, leave the warm tent and refill it. Usually we doused the half-cooked porridge with sugar and milk and downed it.

Lunch inevitably consisted of Knorr soups, which we enjoyed before they became widely known and appreciated in Canada.

They proved tasty and were one of the few items we could not spoil. Chocolate or a chunk of salami or a few sardines rounded out the meal. Stew formed the evening meal. Into a pot of boiling water went the contents of a package of soup. We rooted around in the ration box for extra ingredients to thicken the brew, throwing in bits of biscuits, pieces of meat and other items. Brian added cheese to one pot, creating a new taste sensation – burnt cheese stew. We ate it anyhow. Because we did not wash the pots on a regular basis, each meal carried over its flavour to the next one; the soup tasted of porridge.

Caribou hairs formed a part of every meal, finding their way into every pot, pan and cup. Our wet socks and gloves hanging from the roof of the tent sometimes dripped moisture into the pots. We wiped them out with paper towels or toilet paper but they remained encrusted with past meals. Once a week I'd round up all the pots and pans, heat a basin of water, and wash them. Within a day or two they would be as thick with leftover food as before. The residents of one tent came up with a quick and easy way of keeping their pots clean. They left them near the dogs. This practice ceased when the huskies ran away with the pots and had to be chased. And someone noticed that the dogs cleaned certain parts of their anatomy with their tongues.

On some days, to save fuel, six of us crowded into a tent.

Politeness always prevailed at meals and other times; it is as necessary to the success of a polar expedition as it is to a good marriage. People thanked each other for small courtesies and services. I recall Geoff leaning across me, sticking a filthy hand into the cook pot to grab a morsel, saying: "Please excuse me." At a communal meal, a casual movement would hit someone's arm, his dish would tip and the contents spread over a sleeping bag or caribou skin. After the customary but never resented curse – "clumsy bastard" – the mess would be scraped up, the caribou hairs removed and the food eaten. On May 18, Norwegian Independence Day, Keith made ice cream with dried milk, sugar and water. Left outside the tent to freeze, it tasted delicious. Keith also made a Chinese meal. I watched him balance six pots on the stove at once and the food made a welcome change for us. On his birthday, I made him a special meal – hors d'oeuvres (salami and sardines), leek soup, stew, and strawberry cream pudding, on which I spelled out "Happy Birthday Keith" in spaghetti.

After a while, though, everything from the sardines to the chocolate bars tasted alike. The base camp had an oven and our colleagues sent us up freshly baked bread from time to time; it vanished in a day. Char also helped to break the monotony of our regular meals.

The Defence Research Board used Operation Hazen to test new foods for the military. After the blizzard, Geoff opened a case containing rum-soaked fruit cake developed to sustain downed airmen and others in dire distress. We each ate a piece and agreed that it was too rich for our tastes. The winter party enjoyed the cake, served with cheese, for two months then tired of it. More welcome was the freeze-dried food supplied in 1957. The steaks and pork chops proved so popular that we had freeze-dried chicken and other foods supplied to us in the following year. We fried these delicacies on a piece of tin. As well as tasting delicious, this food, especially the steaks, helped our morale.

You need quick energy on the trail or while working in the Arctic. Our rations included meat, oatmeal and shortbread bars. Meat bars were pounded into crumbs and used in stews or added to soup; we made meat sauce with them. They were gritty and never proved popular. Roger Deane said he planned to write a book entitled "A Thousand Things to do with Meat Bars." We offered our suggestions including striking matches on them. Oatmeal bars left your mouth feeling like a desert if you chewed them; pounded up they made a decent porridge. Shortbread and chocolate bars provided handy snacks at any time; they were stuffed into sledge bags and parka pockets. Like the Inuit, who nibbled on a piece of dried fish or meat while they scoured the land for game, we ate on the hop while doing research on the glacier.

You soon lose interest in sex on polar ventures. To some extent concern about food takes its place. As Greely's men slowly starved to death at Camp Clay on Cape Sabine, some conjured up the magnificent meals they would eat when they returned safely to the south.

As a last resort, if we were starving, we could cut off our parka buttons, which were made of compressed soup, and make a meal from them. The lake party received a batch of edible candles. They came with the baffling directions: "Remember, use these candles sparingly. You cannot light and eat them too."

The Melt Season Arrives

We all remained healthy throughout our stay. Once in a while, one of us would develop a headache or a shiver, but the cold and our squalid living conditions probably deterred any bacteria or viruses from coming near us.

In the early days, we used the stoves for heating the tents as well as for cooking, keeping the tent door closed. Then came that great day when we turned off the stove after cooking a meal as the sun warmed the tent. Leaving the door open at night we arose to the splendid sight of the land below the glacier. And my mouth no longer felt like the bottom of a baby's pram because fresh morning air filled the tent. In 1958 Brian used wood and plastic to make a window for the tent door so we could enjoy the view during the cold days. The weather proved variable. In 1957 the temperature reached 42.1°F (6°C) on June 11. On our warmest day that year the thermometer recorded a maximum of 46.6°F (8°C) around eleven in the morning. Temperatures varied as much as eight degrees in a few minutes as the air above the glacier warmed up and its surface began to melt.

In both years, the melt season began with great suddenness, as if a tap had been turned on up-glacier. In late June streams ran through the camp and life became very wet. Ration boxes and Nutrican cases slid off the skirts of the tents, which rose on ice pedestals. Our living spaces became smaller and smaller as the sheepskins under our sleeping bags absorbed more and more water. From time to time, we emptied the tents, took them down and re-pitched them on a flat part of the glacier. Then the process of "pedestalation" began again. The floor of the Logan tent became icy. One morning, just after the melt began, I crossed a stream to reach it and found the desk holding the recording instruments had slid to the rear of the tent. Slipping and sliding, I dragged it back to its proper place and secured it. On another occasion, at the first observation, I found the Stevenson Screen leaning over, ready to fall. The meteorological mast rose higher and higher as the ice around its base melted. I checked the guy ropes holding it up every day. The mast fell down only once during the time of observations. I determined that the anemometers and thermocouples were undamaged and, with the help of the others, re-erected it. No readings were missed.

I did what I could to divert water from draining through the camp. The May blizzard banked snow behind the tents. It melted, forming mounds of soggy, water-soaked slush. I dug channels to drain the outflow away from the tents; they turned into small lakes in a day or two. Bits of packages, dog crap and other debris became the nucleus of pools. The only benefit from the melt came from no longer having to heat ice to make water. We always went well up-glacier for this water because you never knew where the dogs had strayed in the camp.

The land, so white, bright and pure when we landed, shed its snow and turned black. Pools of water formed in the lee of mountains, even at high elevations, proof of the strong warming power of the sun beyond the eightieth latitude. The glacier surface took on a damaged, rutted look in contrast to the pristine whiteness that prevailed when we arrived. Melt streams wandered through the camp, and we slipped and stumbled around, never sure of our footing, sometimes sinking knee-deep into slush. The conditions during the melt season proved far more trying than the times of intense cold after we arrived.

During the melt season, temperatures on and above the glacier stabilized. From May 18 to August 8, 1957, we enjoyed 1,284.2 hours of sunshine, an average of 15.5 hours a day. The traditional method of measuring sunshine with a card behind a crystal ball proved inadequate because it had been designed for use in lower latitudes, not for service during endless days.

In my three long stays north of eighty, I never saw the sun set. The wind came mainly from the northwest after crossing the frozen, dry interior of northern Ellesmere Island. In early July 1958, we had an unexpected fall of rain on the glacier. This part of Canada, an arctic desert, receives very little snow or rain. Vegetation flourishes where melt waters flow from glaciers and pools form in hollows around Lake Hazen.

We had calm weather about a quarter of the time on the glacier. During the melt season, the clear blue skies of early summer filled with scudding clouds that flattened the light. Great lakes formed at the edges of the Gilman. Hemmed in by dams of ice and snow they would drain when these melted and we heard the thunderous sound of the water flowing towards the lake when this happened. We felt small and humble amid these great natural dramas. By late July, the sun had lost its power to melt the glacier ice as it circled lower and lower in the sky. We determined, from our observations, that air temperatures during June and July were key factors in understanding the regime of the glacier. We had a few snowfalls in July each year, but the white blanket on the melting ice never stayed very long. The surface of the glacier melted at the rate of about a centimetre a day.

By early August, the streams on the glacier had frozen or filled with slush. The sun glinted frostily off the ice and it was easier to walk around the camp and up and down the glacier. About three o'clock on August 8, 1957, while eating lunch in a tent with Geoff and Fraser, I heard a faint "crump." The met mast had fallen down so that ended the glacial meteorological program for the year. I continued to do the thrice daily observations until we left the glacier.

Expedition members travelled extensively over the ice cap and saw parts of Canada that no one had even seen before except from the air. Our ancient and modern sledges stood up to hard travel over ice and snow and during the melt season. The Nansen sleds had "Tufnol" runners of bakelite, a material that travels more effectively over ice than steel. The rough glacier surface smashed two longitudinals and the runner of one sledge, but they were easily repaired. The two clumsy looking Greenland sledges gave us a link to the past, and helped us to appreciate the ingenuity of the early

Inuit. They made their sledges of driftwood and whalebone, lashed together with sealskin, but they looked exactly like the ones we used. Greely found ancient Inuit sledges abandoned on Ellesmere Island and Greenland. Why did the Inuit leave them? They took a great deal of time and scarce resources to make. Abandoning a sledge resembled a rich North American walking away from an expensive car.

Despite our feelings of comradeship, Geoff's inspired leadership and seeing new places while travelling on the sledges and the Eliasons, we still had to cope with the stresses of isolation, cramped living conditions and assorted hardships including living in a water-saturated snow and icescape.

Staying Sane

*"The Arctic expresses the sum total of all wisdom.
Silence. Nothing but silence. The end of time."*
　　　　　　　　　　– Walter Bauer, "Canada" (1968)

The utter and complete silence in the Arctic can overwhelm you. It seems to weigh you down, oppress you at times. In ordinary life we hear all kinds of noises from all kinds of sources. Apart from the roar of melt streams, we heard no sounds on the glacier other than our own voices and the barks and howls of the dogs. I did not share the sense of timelessness of the others, who paid no attention to clock time as they carried out their research. When my regular schedule of observations ended just before we left the glacier for the base camp, I too felt a sense of being out of time, in a kind of void.

Even on a well-planned and equipped venture like Operation Hazen, we all felt a trifle bushed towards the end of the season on the glacier. Work dominated our lives. On bad days, when rain, snow and fog shrouded the glacier, we stayed in the tents, chatting, sleeping, reading. From time to time we'd go for short walks to the edge of the glacier, but really there was not a great deal to see or do there until the melt started. After lakes drained at the eastern edge of the Gilman, they left behind a fantastic variety of ice forms – granular, pitted, honeycombed. We waded into these fields of stranded ice, smashing away with our ice axes, delighting in the sound of the brittle material shattering and disintegrating. Feeling relaxed after this burst of energy, we headed back to the comforting routine of camp life.

Radio reception proved erratic. We could not raise the base camp at times but heard broadcasts from distant lands with startling clarity. Through Stan Surber, a ham radio operator in Peru, Indiana, we sent out messages. He had a daily schedule with High Arctic weather stations and RCMP posts and we all appreciated his dedication to alleviating our isolation. We picked up Radio Denmark and the Voice of Switzerland in 1957. Every time we heard an orchestra, it was playing *Arrividerci Roma* so we concluded it was the only tune it knew. We heard a CBC program on which Svenn Orvig spoke about life on a glacier and eavesdropped on Roger when he contacted the Eureka weather station.

A casual twirl of the dial one day brought in a mass celebrating the eight-hundredth anniversary of the founding of the city of Freibourg in Switzerland. Radio Moscow came in loud and clear. We heard lots of Soviet propaganda, a detailed description of a football match – in English – and a lecture in the same language on romanticism in Ukrainian literature, a topic of little interest to us. But it did help to relieve the monotony of our lives.

We understood the exasperation of a man in the western Arctic who wrote to *The News of the North*, complaining about radio reception. He could never find the standings in the National Hockey League by listening to the radio. But Radio Moscow kept him fully informed on the status of the Leningrad Tram Conductors' Chess Tournament. We caught a sketch on the Goon Show that featured a duel: "Name your weapon!" "I name my weapon – Basil."

The generator that powered our radio never worked very well. It's useful to have a dysfunctional piece of machinery on a polar expedition. People can spend hours trying to fix it while others curse and kick it, relieving pent-up feelings. For reasons that escaped us, Keith, who was studying Russian, decided to name the Eliason toboggans, using the Cyrillic alphabet. He painted "So Near" and "Yet So Far" on the noses of the machines above the Defence Research Board crest. One of these snow toboggans still lies at the base camp, classified as an Arctic artifact. Doubtless visitors will wonder how Russian letters came to adorn a Canadian military machine.

Polar ventures these days have lots of sophisticated technology, including radios with which participants can easily contact the outside world and stay in touch with loved ones. A dying New Zealand climber on Mount Everest reached his wife by satellite phone and spoke his last words to her. A tourist on a dog sledging trip in Nunavut in 1999 began to pass blood. Paul Landry, the guide, phoned a doctor. After hearing details of the man's condition, the doctor suggested Landry monitor him. The tourist felt fine, remained in good health and completed the trip.

What would have happened if early explorers had had such gizmos?

"John Franklin here. Sorry to bother you, but we're in a spot of trouble. Nothing serious, but we would like to see a rescue ship. Could you please oblige? I'm not feeling too well, but the crews are in good spirits. Would be most awfully obliged if you could reach us. Thank you."

"Captain Scott. Sir, I just spoke to that Norwegian bloke. Can't recall his name – foreign sounding. Says he has made it to the South Pole. Not much point in you pressing on, is there, sir. Why not turn round and come back to base, old chap?"

"Lieutenant Greely here. Could I speak with the Secretary of War. We've reached the rendezvous point on Smith Sound. No sign of the relief ship and the men are starving. He's in conference? Alright, I'll hold."

Mail is incredibly important to those in isolation, although letters can create frustration if you are not able to reply to them. We had one or two mail drops at the base camp and on the glacier during Operation Hazen. My friend Otto wrote of the warm summers in Montreal and the wonderful sight of women students lying on the grass of the McGill campus, their breasts pointing skywards. Going north plays hell with your love life. Before leaving Montreal in 1957, I had met a woman who was mildly interested me. She gave me her photo, which I stuck on the side of a box in the tent. In the following year, I had a torrid involvement with the daughter of a Texas millionaire. This affair suffered a setback when her mother discovered us necking on a couch in the family home in North Hatley, Quebec, and sent me packing. During the miserable summer of 1959, Pat's letters helped to keep me sane.

The difficulties of communicating in the Arctic in the past can be appreciated from the tortuous route a letter that Brian Sagar wrote to me in 1959. I was on the Ward Hunt ice shelf, he at the snout of the Gilman Glacier, a hundred and fifty kilometres away.

His letter went to Montreal, thence to New York, on to Thule and was dropped to me.

Fragile relationships come apart when people go north. Bill Marshall, who was with Geoff on the 1954 ice shelf expedition, had particularly bad luck with his women friends. Geoff recalled transcribing a three-hundred-word radio message to him. It said, in effect: "I like you, but I really don't know how I feel about you." Marshall spent a season on Ice Island T-3 floating around the Arctic Ocean. One day, the party received an airdrop. The mail sack buried itself in the ice and had to be dug out by eager hands. Bill expected a letter from his current girlfriend. When he opened it, it proved to be a "Dear John" letter.

I received a similar letter from my Texan girlfriend after a strenuous trip to the snout of the glacier in 1958. Ian Jackson's engagement to a fellow geography student did not survive his year at Lake Hazen. Being a canny Yorkshire lad, he turned his long, long letter to his fiancée into an enjoyable book, *Does Anyone Read Lake Hazen?*.

When in camp, we made our own entertainment, as did our Inuit predecessors. What songs they sang we can never know. Probably, like us, each Inuk had a party piece that he or she performed to delight the others. Our repertoire ranged from the serene to the obscene, and we performed with gusto if not skill. Keith and Hal had mouth organs, and Hans brought along his guitar.

Keith's party piece, "I gotta motta, always merry and bright," was sung in French in a lugubrious tone; it began: *"J'étais toujours un bon garçon. Quelquefois joli et quelquefois non."*

Brian's party piece began: "I went to Gay Paree / And paid five francs to see / A lovely French lady, / Tattooed from head to knee."

Then followed graphic descriptions of the pictures on the lady's anatomy sung in stentorian tones, ending: "And just for swank / She had a German tank / Tattooed where I could not see."

Strumming his guitar, Hans specialized in strange European student songs. The chorus of one went: "Eins a bitten koff / Erts a bitten koff / Der booby, booby, booby koff." We did not understand what we sang, but shattered the glacier's silence as we raised our voices in the choruses. We all joined in *Avanti Popolo*, the anthem of the Italian Communist Party. I offset its revolutionary tone with a British version of "The Red Flag": "The working class/ Can kiss my ass/ I've got the foreman's job at last." My working-class heritage included a vast number of rude jokes and songs. The latter included "The Hole in the Elephant's Bottom," "Please Don't Burn Our Outhouse Down" and "They're Digging Up Father's Grave to Build a Sewer." Hal recalls more sedate offerings: "Local entertainment consisted of lustily sung versions of 'Jerusalem' and 'Ilkley Moor bar-tat' led by Jim Lotz and Keith, as well as 'Fa mal i pe' by Hans."

Shackleton's men made up their own song, and so did we, to the tune of "The Mountains of Mourne":

> They say that the Gilman's a very fine place,
> That the organization's a bloody disgrace.
> There's geophysicists, glaciologists and surveyors too,
> With their hands in their pocket and nothing to do.
> They stand on the ice and they bawl and they shout,
> They shout about things they know nothing about.
> And for all that I've done here I might as well be
> Shovelling shit on the Isle of Capri.

We shared jokes and here I had an advantage, coming from a city where humour eased the strains of change and the interaction between different ethnic groups. It's hard to hate people when you are laughing together.

Knowing I'd be alone for extended periods, I took forty-eight paperback books with me each summer and had the companionship of Zola, Koestler, Gide, Greene, Camus, Rabelais, Mencken, Tawney, Maugham, C.V. Wedgewood, Mann, Brinton, Tacitus, Ovid, Flaubert, Melville, Suetonius, Bertram Wolfe, Gabrielle Roy, and Hugh MacLennan. The Arctic, with few distractions, is an ideal place to absorb new knowledge. However, I remember very little of what I read in those summers, although some of it has stayed with me and influenced my thoughts and actions. Cyril Connolly's word cycle, *The Unquiet Grave*, appealed to me with its observations and aphorisms that I jotted down in my diary. They included:

"The friendships which last are those wherein each friend respects the other's dignity to the point of not wanting anything from him." – Connolly

"Every man is to be respected as an absolute end in himself; and it is a crime against the dignity that belongs to him to use him as a means to some external purpose." – Kant

". . . every man who does not accept the conditions of life sells his soul." – Baudelaire

"Whatever you blame, that you have done yourself." – Groddeck

"The greatest good is the knowledge of the union which the mind has with nature." – Spinoza

An observation by Homer Smith in *Man and His Gods* had particular relevance to our life on the glacier as we did our work amid an eternal presence manifested in silence, in a land unchanged for hundreds, perhaps thousands, of years: "Unhappiness, whether avoidable or not, too frequently comes in large pieces. But happiness is generally as fine-grained as life itself, and so intimately intermixed with living that it cannot be extracted from breathing, eating, sleeping, waking, from the humblest labor, from all achievements of creation and understanding . . . "

Connolly's observations on Ernest Hemingway struck a responsive chord: "The greatness of Hemingway is that he alone of living writers has saturated his books with the memory of the physical pleasures, with sunshine and salt water, with food, wine and making love, and with the remorse that is the shadow of that sun."

We had an odd link with Hemingway. In "The Snows of Kilimanjaro" he writes of the discovery of the dried and frozen carcass of a leopard near the summit of the East African mountain, remarking, "No one has explained what the leopard was seeking at that altitude." Geoff and Hal found muskox bones and a skull at 1,200 metres on the Half Sister, which rose near the Seven Sisters, a line of peaks west of the glacier. We saw fox droppings on the 1,740-metre summit of Mount Nukap. What were these animals doing at such high altitudes? Emerging from the tent one morning, I found the dogs eerily silent and subdued. Looking down glacier, I saw an animal about two hundred metres away. Had one of the dogs broken loose? I counted them; none was missing. Our visitor was a wolf. Greely left his dogs behind when he quit Fort Conger. Had they bred with wolves? Had one of their descendants retained some memory of the time when humans and animals lived together? Did hunger or curiosity drive these animals to these solitary places?

Geoff offered me opportunities to travel away from the glacier and see more of the country in 1957 and 1958, and we spent most of the 1960 season moving around the ice cap. In the first two summers I had to be back in camp by eight in the morning, and could not leave until after ten in the evening in order to maintain my schedule of weather observations.

In June 1958, Geoff and Brian planned an overnight trip to the snout of the glacier to pick up equipment and mail that Dingle Smith would deliver there. I decided to go with them on what looked like an easy four-hour trip and catch up on my sleep on the next day. I looked forward to receiving mail, expecting a letter from my current girlfriend whose affection wavered just before I left Montreal.

This trip proved to be my worst journey.

Brian drove the Eliason with Geoff sitting behind him while I sat on the Nansen sledge. Hummocky ice slowed us down and tipped me off. About a mile from the start of the glacier snout where it began to slope downwards, Geoff went ahead to find an easy route to land. The Gilman had been selected for study because it was easy to ascend and descend; the Henrietta Nesmith Glacier, much nearer the base camp, had a sheer face that made it very inaccessible.

Brian and I unhitched the sledge. He towed it down the glacier snout while I steered, one foot on the brake. The Nansen behaved like a mad thing, sliding, swinging, swerving, throwing off the cargo, acting as if it had a mind of its own. Geoff cheered us by saying that the ice conditions were the worst he had ever encountered. Finally, we left the sledge, put its cargo into backpacks and edged our way down the glacier snout. A thin layer of snow over the ice made walking treacherous. Our feet slid from under us and we grabbed at the ice with our axes to avoid a precipitous descent. As the incline became steeper, Geoff cut steps in the ice. I put my feet in them carefully, steadying myself with my ice axe. At fifty

Brian Sagar (left) and Geoff Hattersley-Smith at the snout of the Gilman Glacier.

metres above ground level, I slipped. Clawing frantically with my axe to stop my rapid descent I slid the rest of the way on my backside. Dingle looked down at me and observed, ""That's not the way to do it!" Geoff politely inquired as to whether my glissade had been voluntary or involuntary. Protected by thick arctic clothing, I suffered no injury except to my dignity.

All through the summer, I had been carrying on imaginary conversations in my head with my Texan girlfriend and writing letters to her in my mind. Sorting through the mail, I found the "Dear John" letter from her. With my difficult descent from the glacier in mind, I thought, "So what!" I put the young lady out of my mind and prepared for the return to the glacier camp. It could not possibly be as difficult and dangerous as our descent down the snout, I thought. I was wrong.

We started the return trip about 5:30 in the morning, in bright sunshine. The sun had already melted the steps Geoff had cut into the face of the glacier. To keep my balance, I held the mail bag in my teeth. Imperturbable as ever, Geoff came behind me as I scrambled up the snout of the glacier. Seeing my distress, he went ahead, hacking steps in the glare ice. At one point, a step collapsed under my foot. Digging in my ice axe, I hung suspended, scared stiff, while my feet frantically sought for a safe footing. We finally reached the flatter parts of the glacier and looked forward to an easy ride home. We dragged our weary bodies over to the Nansen and man-hauled it to the Eliason. Slipping, sliding, cursing, sweating profusely, pausing to catch our breath, we hitched the sled to the machine. Firing up the snow toboggan, we saw it dig itself into the ice. Unhitching the sledge we heaved the Eliason out of the pit dug by the tracks and set it on firm ice. We hitched up the sledge again and started the Eliason. Again the machine moved downwards instead of forwards, digging its tracks into the ice. Although lightly loaded, the Nansen felt as if it weighed a ton as we unhitched it again and pulled the snow toboggan out of its pit.

Finally the tracks of the machine found strong purchase on the glacier ice and we sped towards the camp. I drove. My glasses misted up, as did my snow goggles, and I thought I'd gone snow-blind. My fingers lost all feeling as my sweat-soaked gloves froze. My clothes, encased in ice, felt like body armour. Brian looked like a real Arctic explorer, covered from head to foot in snow, his beard frozen, his face red.

We reached the camp just before eight in the morning. Flinging myself into the nearest tent, I made a cup of coffee and then did the first weather observation before stripping off my sweat-soaked, ice-encrusted clothes. For the next two days, only my brain appeared to be working as I moved my numbed body through the familiar two-hour cycle of instrument reading.

For all its perils, this trip gave us a feeling of kinship with past polar explorers to whom such journeys became routine. We also felt a sense of elation, a certain joy in having completed a hard journey and tested ourselves to our limits. These feelings outweighed all the hardships of the trip.

As we learned more about the glacier, we encountered much that we did not understand. As Albert Schweitzer put it: "As we acquire more knowledge, things do not become more comprehensible, but more mysterious."

Chapter 7

Discoveries and Mysteries

Farewell to Lake Hazen University – a very stimulating intel-
lectual environment!! Many thanks for the hospitality.
— Terris Moore's entry in the visitors' book
at base camp August 7, 1958

Terry Moore, a former president of the University of Alaska, turned up unexpectedly at the base camp in the summer of 1958. He had flown his float-equipped Piper Supercub solo to support a Columbia University expedition on a small ice cap south of Tanquary Fiord and came over to the base camp for a visit. He received a warm welcome from the people at the lake, and placed his plane at the disposal of the scientists. Terry flew 6,600 kilometres in it, saving Bob Christie, Barry Walker and Moreau Maxwell endless hours of footslogging.

This admirable American stayed true to his guiding maxim: "There is no limit to the good a man can do if he doesn't care who gets the credit." He flew to Lonesome Creek, which flows into

Conybeare Fiord, where Max had found one of the richest traces of the ancient Inuit. He picked up Max and brought him back to the base camp for a meal then returned him to the excavation site. Terry took his Supercub through the north-south valley that separates the Grant Ice Cap from the main body of ice to the west; Piper Pass commemorates this flight.

Terry caught the essence of what Operation Hazen became – an outdoor university where we explored an area that offered unparalleled opportunities for pure research. Early expeditions to northern Ellesmere Island focused on the "where" and "what" of research, with exploration and short-term observations of natural phenomenon. Greely stated that the Lady Franklin Bay Expedition had discovered thirteen thousand square kilometres of new land in 1881-83 and achieved the following:

> "1. The satisfactory, if not complete determination of the extent of North Grinnell Land [i.e. northern Ellesmere Island].

> "2. The outlining of the extraordinary and previously unsuspected physical conditions of the interior of the country.

> "3. The discovery of numerous valleys covered with comparatively luxuriant vegetation, which afforded sufficient pasturage for large numbers of musk oxen."

We drew upon the findings of Greely's expedition, but focused more on the "why" and "how" of what we studied. How did this Arctic oasis come into being? How deep was Lake Hazen and what lived in it? How many muskoxen roam this part of Ellesmere Island? What other kinds of wildlife live here? How do they survive the bitter cold? We had similar questions about the vegetation.

At the edge of the Gilman Glacier.

How did the climate of the interior of the island differ from that on the coasts where the weather stations of Alert and Eureka were located? Were the glaciers of northern Ellesmere Island thickening or thinning, advancing or retreating?

We filled in blanks on the map, widened the boundaries of knowledge in a largely unexplored part of Canada, and prepared the way for those who would come after us, whether they be scientists, mountain climbers or tourists. Geoff and Brian discovered a dog sledge route through a high pass at the head of Disraeli Glacier in 1958. In 1967 Geoff and Keith climbed Barbeau Peak, the

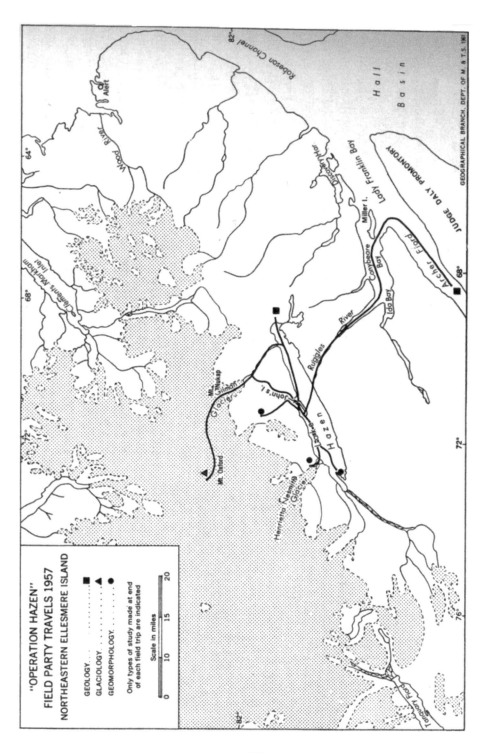

"OPERATION HAZEN"
FIELD PARTY TRAVELS 1957
NORTHEASTERN ELLESMERE ISLAND

GEOLOGY. ■
GLACIOLOGY. ▲
GEOMORPHOLOGY. ●

Only types of study made at end
of each field trip are indicated

Scale in miles

0   10   15   20

highest mountain in Canada east of the Rockies, which rises to 2,505 metres; it's west of the head of Henrietta Nesmith Glacier.

Geoff's research in 1957, 1958 and subsequent years revealed how difficult it can be to determine whether the Arctic is warming, cooling or going through short-term cycles of this. There is no doubt that global warming is taking place. Is this a long-term or a short-term phenomenon? From his studies of the Gilman Glacier, Geoff surmised that, since 1925, it had usually lost more ice during the summer than it gained during the winter as the climate warmed. Five cold summers in 1963-67 reversed this trend. Small changes can have big impacts on the regime of arctic glaciers. During the winter of 1959-60, strong winds blew lots of dust onto the surface of the Gilman. The melt season in 1960 began ten days earlier than in the previous two years as the dust attracted the sun's rays and lessened the albedo. Between 1957 and 1967, the Gilman lost about ten centimetres of ice from its surface.

From the seismic work, Fraser Grant, Hans Weber and their colleagues determined that the Gilman varied in depth from 300 metres five kilometres from its terminus to 760 metres at its head where it flowed out of the ice cap. Soundings there revealed thicknesses of ice varying from 400 to 800 metres. The *nunataks*, isolated peaks rising above the surface, once overlooked valleys carved by streams in the distant past. The ice cap has been thinning since the last ice age, which ended about ten thousand years ago. During this time, huge ice sheets advanced and retreated at least four times as the climate warmed and cooled. Greenland ice spread across Ellesmere Island and merged southwards with the Laurentide Ice Sheet, which covered most of Canada and parts of the United States.

Keith Arnold measured the movement of the glacier by locating lines of bamboo stakes that we drilled into its surface and determining that it was advancing about twenty-five metres a year. Our

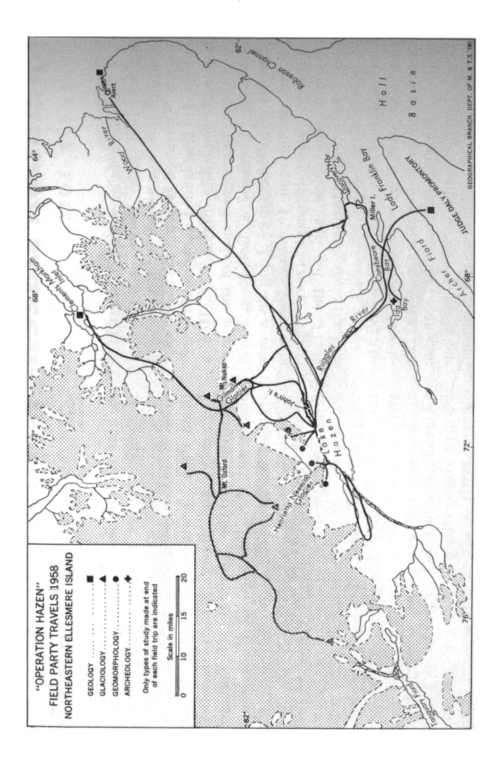

research indicated that the other major glaciers on northern Elles-mere Island had a stable regime; they were not losing much ice each year and were advancing slowly.

Some glaciers behave oddly. The Otto Glacier, which drains into the fiord of the same name on the west coast of Ellesmere, suddenly surged forward in 1950. Its terminus grounded below sea level in the fiord in that year, advancing three kilometres over the next nine years; icebergs calved from its floating snout. The glacier advanced another three kilometres between 1959 and 1964. A flight over the Otto Glacier in July 1963 showed extensive crevassing – a sign of movement – on its lower twenty-five kilometres. The mean height of the glacier did not change. Its horizontal movement aver-aged 7.7 metres a day, but you would not notice this if you were sitting on the glacier.

Each glacier moves to its own geophysical rhythm. Glacier ice is plastic and flows freely under certain circumstances. Exactly what these are still baffles glaciologists. About a thousand years ago, the Hubbard Glacier in Alaska, which drains into Yakutat Harbor, retreated. Around a century ago, it began to advance.

Even during our short stays we experienced great variations in the ice cover of Lake Hazen. In the summer of 1957, the lake level rose a metre in thirty-three days. By the second week of August, the lake was ice-free. In the following year, at around the same time, ice covered about a third of the lake. In the summer of 1959, Lake Hazen remained covered in ice in the middle of August. On May 23, 1960, we landed on the lake ice in a DC-3, but by June 2, it was too unsafe for a plane to land.

Sudden changes have marked Arctic weather in the past and are difficult to explain. Like Greely, we were baffled by the fact that the outlet of Lake Hazen at the head of the Ruggles River remained ice-free all winter, perhaps because of an upwelling of warm water. In 1995, however, with low water levels in the lake, the outlet froze.

The weather on the glacier varied from year to year. In the first seven days of August 1957, I recorded 46 hours of sunshine, 2.4 inches of snow and 0.09 inches of rain. In the same period in the following year we had 165 hours of sunshine and only traces of snow.

Changes in climate can have a dramatic effect on the ice cover and plant and animal life in the Arctic. We were constantly amazed at the tenacity with which life, in all its forms, sustained itself and thrived in this Arctic desert. On the Greely Expedition, Lieutenant Kislingsbury – the man who missed the boat – shot a hare through the hind leg. The animal hopped away with the officer in close pursuit for three kilometres. Kislingsbury put a bullet into its stomach. The hare ran for another three kilometres, losing "a cupful of entrails." The American fired at the animal again, breaking both its forepaws. The animal sought safety by leaping on to a high rock then fell off a seventy metre cliff. When the officer retrieved his prize, the hare still showed signs of life. Kislingsbury also shot a wolf which ran until it fell dead, "his body literally bloodless." A small arctic animal literally outfoxed another member of Greeley's expedition. After Biederbick shot a fox, it lay down. So sure was he of the kill, the soldier did not bother to reload his gun. When he bent to pick up the fox, it leapt up and escaped.

Greely tells a charming story about an encounter with the wildlife of the Lake Hazen basin: "A fine hare, still in fur of perfect white, visited me while I was making my observations and examined me curiously at a distance of a few yards. As I was not armed he escaped, but even had I been, I should have hesitated about killing an animal which, having such natural timidity, had placed so much confidence in my kind intentions."

Muskoxen grazing around Lake Hazen.

When officers from the US Coast Guard Cutter *Eastwind* visited the base camp in August 1957, a weasel looked them over then went about its business. Even the north coast of Ellesmere Island nurtures animal life. A weasel we named Harold dug a burrow under a hut on Ward Hunt Island. We found a pair of antlers on the island and the corpse of a white fox that apparently died of starvation. Frank returned to the camp one day with stories about a huge rabbit – "as big as a wolf" – that he had encountered. Arctic hares can weigh five kilograms fully grown but they are never that big.

Muskoxen, always on the move, feed on the sparse ground cover. In 1973, an autumn storm with freezing rain hit Bathurst Island, forming an unbreakable crust over the vegetation. Unable to paw through this, muskoxen starved and died. These losses were small compared to the wholesale slaughter of these animals that took place when human hunters came to Ellesmere Island.

The US Army chose Fort Conger as a base for the Greely Expedition because of reports from the 1875-76 Nares Expedition of the abundance of muskoxen nearby that would serve as a handy food supply. When attacked by wolves, muskoxen form a circle or a line to protect themselves. This united front deterred wolves but doomed the animals when they confronted men with high-powered rifles. Greely's men and Peary and his Inuit killed hundreds of the great beasts.

John Tener, our mammologist, had a permit to shoot two muskoxen for scientific purposes. The base camp dined on one. We had some of it after we reached the lake in August 1958 and the meat tasted like top quality beef with no hint of "muskiness." John illustrated the expedition's ethics when a party of VIPs flew into base camp. He noted: "I was asked (ordered?) to shoot a muskox for the table." For John, this was the lowest point of his time with Operation Hazen. He shot an old bull for the visitors: "You can be sure I extracted every bit of scientific information [from it] I could . . . I chose an old bull for two reasons: its life would not last much longer anyway, and it would give the VIPs something to chew on!"

John estimated about four thousand muskoxen lived on Ellesmere Island, about a quarter of the total in the Arctic Islands. He and Bob Christie sighted eight Peary caribou in the summer of 1958 – the only other large animal in the High Arctic. It derives its name from the explorer who shot ninety of the smallest caribou in Canada between 1905 and 1909.

Wolves presented no threats. On a journey from the glacier to the base camp, John Filo encountered several wolves which cut out one of his dogs; it turned up later at the base camp, slightly bitten but otherwise unharmed. The next party that left camp bristled with rifles and "looked like a bloody army," as someone put it. In August, a wolf loped towards the base camp. To drive the animal away, Hal took a potshot at it. The animal bounded away, stopped and looked back at us. "Come back," we shouted. It did so. Another warning shot, well wide of the animal, did not deter it – the animal just kept looking at us. After a few minutes, the wolf decided we were of no interest and headed for the hills. The animals were curious, never dangerous, although a muskox chased Dick off its turf. Walking to the lake in August 1958, I spotted a herd of muskoxen grazing on a plateau so headed down a valley to avoid it. Halfway along the valley, I looked up to see a large muskox gazing down at me in lofty disdain.

Around the lake we found the skulls and bones of muskoxen killed by hunters. They encouraged lush plant growth by releasing nitrogen. By dying, these large animals aid the growth of new life on the tundra. Their bones trap plant litter and soil particles blown by the wind, creating tiny oases where new vegetation gains a start.

Life explodes in the short summer. Birds come north for the meagre bounties offered by this harsh land. Black and white snow buntings circled the tents on the glacier and the trailer on the ice shelf. Snow Goose River, which flows into Lake Hazen near the base camp, commemorates the presence of these beautiful birds. John Tener identified eighteen different species of birds, recording new northern breeding sites for Baird's Sandpiper and the Lapland Longspur. To date, thirty-five species of birds have been seen in northern Ellesmere Island. We found a ptarmigan's nest in the heart of the ice cap and a flock of twenty-five of these birds settled on Ward Hunt Island in 1959, becoming quite tame. Even hardy birds have problems in this environment; only one pair of snow geese in the Lake Hazen basin raised young in 1958. Knots cavorted and courted in the air while jaegars and snowy owls scanned the ground for lemmings.

We saw signs of one of the great dramas of the Arctic which demonstrate the interrelationships between living things. In 1957, those at the base camp saw thousands of lemmings. In the following year, John trapped only thirty-two of the creatures in ten days. The animals feed on the ground cover and their predators – birds, wolves and foxes – feed on them. The population "crashes" and in the following year the lemming eaters also fall in numbers. The lemmings then breathe – and breed – more freely and their numbers increase. This cycle goes on, year after year. The droppings of the birds and the animals that feed on the lemmings fertilize the soil and encourage new plant growth on which the small creatures live.

Since the ice left the land, plants have adapted to short summers and long winters, bursting into life as the sun rises in the sky and warmth floods the land. Roger found mushrooms near the base camp; one measured twenty-five centimetres in diameter and weighed three quarters of a kilogram. In 1958, John Powell and Jim Soper photographed, collected and dried over a hundred different plants. Northern Ellesmere Island has one hundred and twenty species of vascular plants; Jim and John identified range extensions for sixteen of them. Mosses also flourish in this remote part of Canada in one hundred and sixty varieties. With less than two and a half centimetres of rain, and hummocky barrens, rocky hills and stoney ridges offering no sustenance for vegetation, plants have difficulty finding places to survive and thrive. Patches of tundra and wet meadows with a southeasterly orientation watered by streams from glaciers offer the best locations for vegetation. Dryas, willow, sedges and other plants grow here, and cotton grass waves on the shores of Lake Hazen.

Cotton grass adorns the shores of a lake with the Gilman Glacier in the background.

John made a valiant effort to grow vegetables on a test plot near the base camp, planting beans, peas, carrots, radishes, lettuce, parsley, mustard and cress just after the temperature rose above freezing. The radishes, lettuce and cress poked their heads above the thin soil and tried to complete their life cycles in two months. John watered them regularly but they gave up the struggle and withered away. The base camp at Lake Hazen lies 3,200 kilometres north of the site of Schefferville where I failed to grow vegetables and grain on a test plot in 1956. Both places have the same number of frost-free days.

In midsummer, I jumped on the land east of the glacier camp and spotted a clump of yellow Arctic poppies, purple saxifrage and sorrel growing amid a heap of shattered rock. Seeing this evidence of life flourishing in such a hostile place, my heart filled with the joys of spring, winter and fall. I picked a poppy and stuck it in my balaclava, recognizing a sudden kinship with nature – and what separated me from it. I would quit this land in a month's time. The poppies would die back at summer's end, remain dormant over the winter and come to life again next summer. This mysterious process would continue to repeat itself, year after year, as we went about our ways in the south of Canada.

John visited the glacier camp to help with the work and examine plants on the *nunataks* and the ice-free land at the edge of the glacier. He identified thirty-five plants living on *nunataks* and patches of loose rock. Arctic poppies and saxifrage flowered above 1,400 metres. Lichen splashed rocks with colour at even higher levels and some thrived on and under glaciers. Moss grew in crevices at 2,500 metres and lichen at several hundred metres beyond this limit.

The Arctic has over a thousand species of lichen, a remarkable life form that colonizes places where no others can survive. Lichen consist of algae and fungi; neither can live without the other, and there is no trace of them in the fossil record. They present a mystery. Is the relationship between the two life forms mutually beneficial – or does one exploit the other in a parasitical manner? Why did lichen move further and further north after the last ice age, expanding into places where nothing else grows? Lichen prepare the way for other forms of vegetation. Acid in the fungus breaks down solid rock into usable minerals as the alga turns the sun's energy into chlorophyll to sustain both plants. It can take hundreds of years for lichen to cover a small patch of rock. Single plants lie dormant for decades, waiting for the right moment to send out spores and grow in new places. Ellesmere Island has one hundred and eighty-six species of this remarkable form of life.

Insect life emerged during the summer. Mosquitoes proved a pest in the wet parts of the Lake Hazen basin. They even flourished off the north coast of Ellesmere Island. Paul Walker, the glaciologist on the ice shelf expedition, claimed to have suffered the most northerly insect bite in Canada on a reconnaissance between Cape Nares (83° 06' N) and Cape Albert Edward (83° 07' N). I bumped into a fly – or vice versa – on the Gilman, the only insect I encountered there. Bright butterflies flitted around the lake and bees pollinated the small struggling flowers to ensure their survival.

Ian McLaren determined that only Arctic char live in the lake, feasting on plankton and phytoplankton. Ian hauled up a great deal of this and caught 670 char, one of which weighed 3.5 kilos, for study. The fish then made delicious eating. In 1995 and 1996 another group of scientists caught and tagged 117 char to determine their pattern of movement in the lake. The fish stay there and do not venture down the Ruggles River to the sea.

Roger Deane's survey of Lake Hazen revealed its greatest depth of 263 metres between Johns Island and the outlet to the Ruggles River. The lake becomes shallow at both ends with depths of fourteen metres in the east and five metres in the west. The Turnabout River drains from the glacier of the same name, follows a meandering path in the lowlands at the eastern end of the lake and warms up considerably before entering it; its temperature rose to 12.6°C in the summer. Glacial melt streams, like the one issuing from the Gilman, pour cold water into Lake Hazen; their summer temperatures do not rise above 3°C. Roger could not explain how this arctic lake formed, but surmised that it had been gouged out by glaciers. Faults in the rock may have aided the process of lake formation.

At the end of the 1958 season, John Tener, Geoff and I visited the outlet of the lake. Here Greely discovered an ancient Inuit dwelling, removing several bone and ivory tools from the site and leaving a tin can. Moreau Maxwell unearthed an ancient tragedy here. The first house had been built around 1300, abandoned and then occupied again twenty-five years later. Whoever lived here at that time only spent a winter at the site. Gravel from the lake, driven by strong winds, covered the house and an ice dyke split it. Each new resident rebuilt the house. Max had to dig down a metre to retrieve artifacts as, at one time, the lake level had been lower than the present one.

Around 1400, a man and a woman spent three years here, living in the house during the winter and in a tent in the summer. The man was older than the woman and, by the standards of the time, the couple was wealthy, owning two sledges with wooden runners and iron tools probably acquired from Norse traders. Temperatures dropped to below -40°C in the winters that the couple spent at the head of the Ruggles River. From a confused mixture of stones, boulders, scraps of wood, pieces of ivory and fur and bones Max determined the fate of the two Inuit. The man died. The woman dragged him to the centre of the summer tent, which was supported by a three-metre tall centre pole and one-metre high side poles around its edge. Then she entered the winter house, ate the dogs and starved to death.

All the woman's precious possessions, including an amber necklace and an ivory comb, lay on the sleeping platform with her bones and those of the dogs. Who had made this jewellery? Why had an elderly man brought a young woman to live with him in the house on the Ruggles? Who had occupied the house before the couple? Had the woman been stolen – or had the couple been sent into exile by their people? Was the man a shaman, an *angakok*, who came to this remote and empty place to commune with the spirits that danced in the sky? Why had the woman died as she did, instead of returning to her people? Field parties found tent rings, fox traps and other signs of the first dwellers around Lake Hazen. Max investigated thirty-three sites, ranging from a "metropolis" at Lonesome Creek (it's named after a dog), which flows into Conybeare Fiord, with forty-three distinct structures to a single tent ring. The house on the Ruggles yielded harpoon heads, wooden dolls, knives, arrowheads, a hundred amber beads and other items. One small artifact bridged the centuries between its long-dead owner and us. Max showed us an ivory needle case with tiny teeth marks on it. Someone in the distant past had used the case as a pacifier for a teething child in the same way that we as parents sometimes grab something to quiet our crying children. Max believed the needle case came from Alaska. But how did it reach northern Ellesmere Island?

Here again, as in so many other areas, we confronted a mystery. Geoff and Keith discovered the most northerly dwelling in Canada when they stumbled over a tent ring in a valley beyond the Seven Sisters Peak. Max identified several stone houses near the lake, one of which had been built by Peary's hunters. He called the Lake Hazen basin a "cultural cul de sac." The ancient Inuit followed the Muskox Way that leads from the head of Tanquary Fiord to the interior of the island. Some of them settled here to hunt muskoxen and other animals. But they soon left.

It's easy to see why they did so.

Ian Jackson's research revealed that the Lake Hazen basin becomes a sink of cold air in winter. Calm air and light breezes prevail here in this season while the weather on the coasts of the island is much more turbulent. The winter party at Lake Hazen recorded temperatures below -55°C on seventy-three days, with an absolute minimum of -55.8°C. Temperatures below -40°C were recorded in every month between October and April. In January 1958, the temperature at the base camp rose to 3°C, strong winds stripped twenty-five centimetres of snow from the land and rain fell at Alert. Ian noted, "It was the only significant meteorological event of the year." Greely experienced a similar January storm at Fort Conger.

And yet, in the past, this part of Canada has been warm. In 1960, Geoff and I sat sunning ourselves on a *nunatak* in the heart of the ice cap. I picked up a curiously shaped rock and showed it to Geoff. It was fossilized coral; the scree slope was strewn with it. At some time in the past, corals had grown in a warm sea in a tropical land. The coal found near Fort Conger and around Lake Hazen had once been tropical vegetation. Four fossil forests have been discovered on Ellesmere and Axel Heiberg Islands; at one site a dawn redwood retained its woody appearance. The trees date from the Eocene Period, between sixty-five and forty million years ago, after the dinosaurs disappeared and the earth began to cool. At one time, northern Ellesmere Island had been a primeval swamp inhabited by large lizards, constrictor snakes, tortoises, alligators, tapirs and flying lemurs. A creature resembling a rhinocerous left its remains in a fossil forest on the northeast coast of Axel Heiberg Island.

In April 2006, the journal *Nature* carried a report on the discovery of fossils of a creature that lived about 375 million years ago in southern Ellesmere Island. Bits of *Tiktaalik roseae* resembled a fish, others a land animal.

How did a warm land with redwood forests, deciduous trees on flood plains and upland boreal forests become an icy desert? How did the creatures here adapt to long periods of darkness? The lava deposits above the fossils offer one possible explanation. Worldwide volcanic activity could have released huge quantities of CO_2 (carbon dioxide), making the Arctic warm enough for cold-blooded creatures to thrive. This gas is high on the list of suspects responsible for global warming in our time.

The iron tools that Max found at the house on the Ruggles River included a drill. They raise intriguing questions about the Norse presence in the High Arctic. Did these wanderers reach Ellesmere Island during the Medieval Warm Period? Or did trading networks take metal artifacts to the Lake Hazen basin? Peter Schledermann, an archeologist who has excavated in eastern Ellesmere Island, believes that Norseman may have reached Smith Sound at least once around 1250-1300, making them the first European "discoverers" of Ellesmere Island.

In all our time in the High Arctic, we never lost our sense of wonder about this remote land. The sky changed constantly. Cottony cumulus rolled over the glacier, followed by altocumulus that sat atop mountains like a stack of pure white plates. The sun turned into a grey blob in fog and low cloud. Then, quite suddenly, it broke through, touching the high clouds with gold, painting the shawls on the mountain slopes in pastel colours. After a June storm on the ice shelf, stratus clouds dissipated, revealing a scene of breathtaking beauty. High cirrus clouds danced across the sky, rippling like the sands of a celestial sea. As lower clouds billowed over the Challenger Mountains, a halo rimmed the midnight sun and the high clouds turned pink. As the sun slipped lower in the sky in September, the wind slashed the omnipresent fog into scarlet ribbons under a fiery red firmament.

On brilliant, bright days on the Gilman, the mountains around and behind us stood out with startling clarity, the air sparkled and the whole world appeared newly born. You felt as if you could reach up into the clear blue sky and touch the hand of God. The fog that sometimes enshrouded the camp felt like a living presence. Thin mists moved up and down the glacier, changing colour as sunlight spread through them. Sometimes thick and clammy, at other times mere wisps of cloud, the fog on the glacier and the ice shelf made you feel utterly isolated and alone, making the everlasting silence there even deeper. Shout into this shrouded world and the words fell into an emptiness as they left your mouth. Even the dogs, usually lively in camp, seemed subdued in this noiseless world. You cannot travel in fog – it destroys your sense of direction, distance and time, making you feel trapped like flies in amber, caught in a world that has lost its momentum. On some days, the fog stayed below the glacier camp. Suddenly it would roll forward and cover the tents like death coming for an old man. In 1960, Geoff and I watched two arms of mist creep up the glacier sides as if seeking to catch us in its embrace. Fogs stayed for days on the ice shelf, even when Ward Hunt Island remained free of it and we could see blue sky above the trailer. Fog bows – known as "fog eaters" by the Inuit and as "sea dogs" by sailors – moved around us, following the sun, like portals to another world. Once I saw a double fog bow. The fog left beautiful luminous crystals on smooth surfaces.

It's easy to see why Peary and Cook saw land that did not exist in the Arctic Ocean. From the Ward Hunt Ice Shelf in early September, the pack ice of the Arctic Ocean looked close enough to the trailer to touch. I drove with John Grady to the edge of the ice shelf and looked over the jumbled masses of ice that stretched for miles. White skyscrapers loomed on the near horizon and we could not tell whether they were bergs, mirages or clouds.

Mountains danced in broken shapes at the head of the Gilman Glacier, phantom lakes appeared to the southwest and imaginary ranges rose in the sky. Wondrous sights lay at the edge of the

Gilman, in the lee of Mount Nukap. The landscape changed daily as the melt advanced, releasing huge quantities of water from the ice. Lakes formed between the land and the glacier. Rivers flowed into and out of them, swirling between glassy-green banks. We jumped over this channel and looked up at huge amphitheatres of dirt and rock deposited by the glacier in the past.

The winter party, like Greely and his men, saw strange celestial phenomenon. Meteors, eclipses, aurora, mirages, luna haloes, paraselinae (mock suns) and the rare *fata organa* illuminated the sky. In this last form of mirage, named for Morgan le Fay, King Arthur's fairy sister, objects appear vertically elongated. Yellow light suddenly flooded the eastern sky and at times the western horizon glowed cherry red. It is easy to understand why the Inuit believed that spirits lived in the sky, watched over them, played tricks and cavorted through the long winter night.

Always I had a sense of awe, a feeling of both powerfulness and powerlessness that came unbidden. Words in *Moby Dick* reflected my mood on many days of solitude or when I travelled across the ice cap: "But not yet have we solved the incantation of this whiteness, and learned why it appeals with such power to the soul . . . Is it that by its indefiniteness it shadows forth the heartless voids and immensities of the universe?"

Each time I left the Gilman and the base camp at the end of the season, I felt as if some part of me remained behind in that lovely, empty land at the edge of Canada. This icy desert, this Arctic Eden, had a sense of enduring permanence. We saw it change during the short summer and realized that it was not as it was now hundreds and thousands and millions of years ago. We had discovered a great deal about it – and about ourselves. But we also recognized how little we really knew and realized we had to continue our explorations in the external world of the Arctic and the internal world of our own being. But, for a short time, we had been privileged to live in a pristine wilderness and to experience a world that few other humans would ever visit. The sense of awe and wonder that I felt when I jumped out of the Flying Boxcar onto Lake Hazen in late April 1957 stayed with me as I prepared to leave at the end of each summer.

And it is with me still.

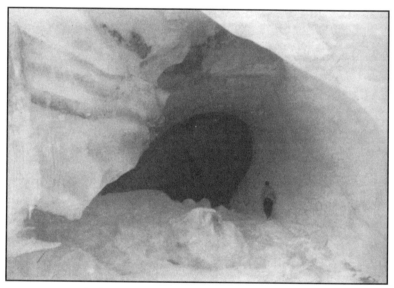

An ice cave at the edge of the Gilman Glacier.

Chapter 8

Departures

This place is somehow out of this world. A sensitive visitor is purified by breathing its air, and feels almost weightless when facing the boundless horizon. He feels himself a clumsy intruder, and is anxious to leave – yet a pilgrim who has reached a shrine and is willing to stay forever.

— Josef Svoboda on Lake Hazen

When I arrived at Lake Hazen in 1957 and 1958 I wanted to leave as soon as possible. Slowly, but surely, this empty land worked its charms on me, and I came to relish its immensity, majesty and stillness. They exalted and dwarfed me, made me aware of great powers in the universe that touched me at the deepest levels.

Doug Wilkinson travelled and made films in the Arctic in the 1950s. He recorded his sense of awe and wonder as the sun returned to North Baffin Island. Red light raced across the sky, chasing dark shadows from the land. The sight stirred "forces deep within me about which I was only vaguely conscious . . . I felt detached from earth." He felt no earthly power could produce such beauty: "I stood in the presence of God . . . and felt his hand on my throat."

I experienced the same emotions on the Gilman Glacier and the ice shelf. Alone on the Gilman, I understood why deserts lure hermits and recluses seeking closer contact with God. Solitude and silence can drive you mad – or open the door to transcendental experiences. The traditional images of polar explorers – faces covered in ice, struggling against the elements, confronting dangers and suffering indescribable hardships – obscure the deeper meaning of time spent in the cold deserts of the world. Like so many before us, we went north in search of something more than adventure.

Apsley Cherry-Garrard wrote about "the negation of materialism" and the freedom from the "bondage of possessions" during his stay in Antarctica. With life reduced to its simplest elements, you must confront your own being at its greatest depths, learn to live with yourself and relish the comradeship of others. Cherry-Garrard observed: "The transcendent beauty of the Antarctic has always awakened a deep sense of wonder in the human spirit. The scale, the purity, the unownedness, these are characteristics that stimulate contemplation."

Shackleton noted: "The stark polar lands grip the hearts of men who have lived on them in a manner that can be hardly understood by people who have never got outside the pale of civilization."

In these solitudes, it's easy to see why early humans feared and worshipped the high and empty places of the world. On the Gilman, Keith invited me to look through a transit trained on the sun. From its surface shot a huge solar flare, like the hand of God reaching into the void. On the ice we rejoiced in the cry of birds and marvelled at sun-seeking plants blossoming in remote places.

Leaving this land generated ambivalent feelings. We wanted to be away but at the same time felt oddly attached to the wilderness in which we had lived for a few months. I left the Gilman Glacier and the base camp in three different ways in 1957, 1958 and 1960.

In 1957, Geoff and I, the last to leave, secured the tents and headed down the glacier over pitted and honeycombed ice, staggering like drunks. I stepped into a hole, soaking my sock and boots. I changed my sock, walked forward and put my foot in another water-filled hole. Melt streams raced down the glacier snout so we strapped on crampons and headed for the side of the glacier where snowbridges linked it to the land. Selecting one, we wondered if it would bear our weight. I was leading Grey. Suddenly the dog lunged forward, eager to reach land. Off went my snow goggles and pack and Grey's pack. The snowbridge held and we relaxed on the land before heading for the glacier snout where a cache of food had been laid for us on the other side of the Gilman River.

Slinging our packs over one shoulder in case the river pulled us off our feet, steadying ourselves with ski poles, Geoff and I plunged into the ice-cold water that came up to our thighs.

Then the trek to Lake Hazen began.

The twenty-kilometre walk took us twelve hours as we crossed ridge after ridge. My soaked feet and ill-fitting boots made every step agony. Eager to reach the lake, we munched chocolate bars, never stopping to prepare a meal. We found a tent at the mouth of the Gilman River with a canoe and motor parked nearby. Gulping down food, we put the canoe in the water and headed west to the base camp thirty kilometres away; we could not have made the journey on foot.

The US Coast Guard Cutter *Eastwind*, which lay at the head of Chandler Fiord, took us out and brought in the winter party. The ship had recently set a new record for a furthest north in the Arctic Ocean. Its helicopters brought in thirty tons of supplies for John Powell, Dick Harington, Ian Jackson and Dingle Smith, who would live in complete isolation for eight months. The four winterers had no idea just how isolated they would be. The crew of the *Eastwind* donated some supplies of dubious value. A sailor put a bag of two-inch nails in one helicopter load and had to be dissuaded from adding a six foot length of chain to it. The ship's doctor visited the base camp and left a box of medical supplies. The four residents had no time to check it. When they did so, they discovered that one fifth of the contents consisted of small bottles and containers labelled "tincture of hydrofluorate" and other designations with no directions for use; the rest consisted of five thousand venereal disease pills.

Geoff forewarned the winterers before we left in August, 1957: "You'll be cursing Ottawa after we've gone." And he was right. Ian Jackson noted that "We were all very glad to get rid of [the 1957 summer party]" so they could settle into a routine. The radio failed after two months and the party had problems with the stove and the heater. The four men, however, survived the winter in good condition, physically and mentally. A psychiatrist sent to check their mental health wrote in the base camp guest book: "I don't know who changed most: them in a winter or me in a week."

The *Eastwind* sailed down Chandler Fiord, into Conybeare Fiord, and across Lady Franklin Bay. At three in the afternoon all hands mustered on deck and saluted as the ship passed the site of Fort Conger. The cutter sailed south through Hall Basin, down

Kennedy Channel and into Kane Basin. Restless and unable to sleep, I walked round and round the ship's deck as the bows of the *Eastwind* smashed through the ice. Huge floebergs rose ahead of the cutter, heaved over and rolled over like great white whales diving into the ocean. New ice in the leads sang a strange sea symphony as the vessel sliced through them. Gazing at the bleak and barren cliffs of eastern Ellesmere Island which dwarfed the ship, I felt a surge of admiration for those who had passed this way in small ships, questing north, unaware of the perils that lay ahead. These icy seas still had bite; the *Eastwind* lost a propeller on the journey from Chandler Fiord to Thule.

The crew of the cutter treated us – and the dogs – royally, lavishing us with excellent food served by attentive Filipino stewards, showing us movies in the wardroom twice a day, and giving us free rein of the ship. We stopped at Alexandra Fiord to disembark Pete Sims, an RCMP officer nicknamed Sergeant Preston by the crew. We went ashore and walked up to the glacier behind the police post. I heard a sailor say to his mate: "Them guys is crazy. They spend their summer freezing their butts on a glacier. Then they go and climb another."

One of the ship's light helicopters crashed on a hill overlooking the police post. The pilot was not hurt and one of the Piasecki helicopters lifted out the aircraft's engine. The captain asked us if we could recover the fuselage. Delighted to be able to do something to return the ship's hospitality, we donned our arctic gear and carried the helicopter's frame down to the ship's boat. The captain gave us a drink of rum, for medicinal purposes as the ship was dry. From the hilltop where the chopper had crashed, Geoff pointed to Pim Island, where Greely and his men spent the starvation winter of 1883-84.

Dropping off the dogs at Kanaq, the *Eastwind* docked at Thule and we flew home from there. Americans cooperated with great efficiency and generosity throughout Operation Hazen, contributing much to the success of the expedition.

As I packed up my gear and equipment and left the glacier in 1958, a great wave of sadness passed over me, for I did not expect ever again to return to this enchanted land and to have such comradeship as I'd experienced in my two Arctic summers.

The scene on the glacier matched my mood. Fog and rain drifted over the camp, the sun vanished behind low cloud, the light became flat, shadows disappeared and the whole place seemed drained of colour. Keith, Brian, Hans and Hal left before Geoff and me, taking the dogs with them. At 4:30 in the afternoon, Geoff and I took one last look around the glacier camp, checked that everything had been secured and set off. We looked at the stakes measuring the melt as we walked down the Gilman. Three swiftly flowing melt streams lay between us and one row of stakes. We put on crampons and leapt across their glassy-green banks. Then we headed for the land at the side of the glacier. Crossing one stream, my crampons hooked together and I barely made it across; Geoff thought I'd had it and expected me to end up in the stream. A slight slip and I would have gone into that swirling water and over the glacier snout and to the ground below – with fatal consequences.

We slipped and slid over the banks of wet scree at the side of the glacier, and finally reached *terra firma*; as Geoff put it, "The more firmer, the less terror." Wading across the Gilman River below the snout we retrieved pots and pans and a stove from a cache then made camp. We found a *Gilman Glacier Gazette* left by Brian, outlining the easiest route to Lake Hazen via Mesa Creek to the west. Brian's screed also included some caustic remarks about the dogs he had with him. Setting up our tent, I squeezed water out of my socks and tipped it out of my boots. Damp, uncomfortable, tired and shoulder-sore I felt on top of the world. On the next morning, Geoff and I measured the snout of the glacier, sloshing around in knee-high, icy water.

Then we set off for the lake. The weather improved and we made good time cutting down a dry valley with sandstone cliffs. Geoff's boots gave him trouble, and mine raised a blister on one toe. Heading down Mesa Creek, I soon reached the lake. Here I found a curious document whose whimsical tone reflected the essence of life on Operation Hazen:

"We are a Swede and a Goth, part of a larger expedition, sent to find His long missing subjects by the King of the Swedes. We have left our companions camped about one day's journey to the west, and have come here (Sonntag) to pick up our sea nets. We have found them full of great seafish and are assured of food for the winter which must come. We have found that the hills here abound with great cattle which are very difficult to kill, but some have fallen to our spears. Three days ago, the bulk of our men was captured by powerful seafaring warriors, and now probably they lie red with blood and [are] dead. Winter will be less hostile to us now that we are reduced to so few. For you who remain of the many who went up to the great land ice we have left food here to cheer you until we return on the morrow as planned. Do not be alarmed at the strangeness of this food, for it was captured from the seafarers of whom we have written and is of a quality which surpasses anything we can wrest from this hostile land. Ave Maria – I.M. [Ian McLaren] J.T. [John Tener]"

An RCAF Canso prepares to leave Lake Hazen, August 1958.

I bolted down some food, pitched the tent, collected dwarf willow and started a fire. Geoff smelled it from a distance and arrived an hour later, limping, cursing his boots. The sky cleared and we lay back, not talking, simply soaking up the solitude of this lovely land. After a good night's sleep, we made a fire, heated some soup and waited for the Swede and the Goth. On the dot of noon, they arrived in a cargo canoe. We climbed aboard in our filthy clothing; our two companions handed us parkas and said we did not smell too badly. Ian threw out a line and caught two Arctic char for lunch, our first fresh food in many weeks.

The US Coast Guard Cutter *Atka* had evacuated the rest of the party and taken them to Thule. An RCAF Canso would arrive for us in a few days' time. Life at the base camp felt idyllic. Ian cut my hair and I took a bath in a tin tub, shaved and felt newly born. We dined on muskox steaks and talked of many things: our work, conservation, our Inuit predecessors, the weather on and off the glacier. It had been a glorious summer for all of us, rich in research results and marked by easy comradeship. I processed about a hundred letters for collectors of polar mail who sent envelopes to be stamped with the expedition's cachet. Geoff knew a man in Antarctica who made £30,000 by stamping mail for collectors.

Roger Deane had stayed behind with Ian McLaren and John Tener and we busied ourselves by tidying up the camp. We walked to the delta of the Snow Goose River, where Dingle Smith had found a strange phenomenon, to examine two kinds of ice on a slumping river bank. One looked like glacial ice; on top of it lay lake ice. Had a glacier advanced from the ice cap some twenty kilometres away and reached the lakeshore at some time in the past? Had the lake level then risen and spilled out over the glacier ice? Here again, as in so many places in this unknown land, we confronted a mystery.

We fell into a limbo state waiting for the plane. The RCAF crew had left some Peary's Peril behind, which we mixed with peach juice to make a potent drink, becoming drunker and drunker in the most blissful manner. The summer party had built a pyramid of junk before they left. Roger, Ian and I staggered out of the hut. Roger poured gasoline on the pyramid with an unsteady hand then lit it. The mountain of trash went up with a wonderful "whoosh!" We danced around the pyre, hooting and hollering, like pagans celebrating the return of the sun. Though this sort of behaviour is not common among academic scientists, it seemed to be the right one for this time and this place. The three of us watched as the flames flickered out, made sure the fire was out then staggered to bed. On August 20, we hauled in a net left overnight and brought in seventeen char. Ian showed me how to gut and clean them and they made a fine feast.

We were living as once the Inuit did, relying on the bounty of the lake. Clouds danced over the ice cap in the crystal clear air and all around the lake the shores blazed with purple saxifrage. Snow geese honked in the distance; like us they were preparing to head south. We nailed up the door of the hut and Geoff left a message on it, inviting anyone who came here to help themselves to whatever they needed. Sitting on our gear, we said little, busy with our thoughts as we prepared to reenter Canadian society. The Canso arrived on time; the crew fished as we boarded the plane. The pilot taxied the plane into the lake, revved the engine and lifted the plane off the water. Firing the JATO (Jet Assisted Take Off) pods, the pilot headed for Thule.

Through the courtesy of a friend of Hans Weber, we visited Camp Century, a scientific base on the Greenland ice sheet. Here I saw the future shape of research on weather in the Arctic– a $25,000 automatic recording device. Geoff let us decide how we wanted to return south. We had authority to travel on MATS (Military Air Transport Services) and some of the party left Thule this way. Their plane landed at Goose Bay, where bad weather grounded it for a week; Jim Soper caught a cold, the only illness any of us suffered on Operation Hazen. Keith stayed with the *Atka*; John, Hans and Max caught a lift on an RCAF Lancaster visiting Thule. Four of us decided to stay with the Canso, stopping at Shephards Bay, a DEW Line station, and Parry Harbour in the western Arctic before landing at RCAF Namao in Alberta, where we caught a plane on a training flight to Winnipeg. After a night there we flew to Ottawa.

Harwood awaited us in the bar at the Lord Elgin Hotel, looking mightily pleased with himself. By any standard, Operation Hazen had been a success, an outstanding contribution by Canada to the International Geophysical Year. The Russians put on an exhibition on the expedition in Moscow; people there probably knew more about it than most Canadians.

We said our final farewells in Ottawa and went our separate ways to work up our data. At the end of my contract I decided to break into the magazine business but the only job offer came from the advertising manager of *The Montrealer*. On the day before I began to walk the streets of the city, I went skiing and broke my ankle. And so began my next Arctic summer with the Canada-US Ellesmere Island ice shelf expedition. I returned to Montreal in September and Pat and I married in December 1959.

After completing my contract with the Arctic Institute, I again found myself unemployed and Pat was pregnant. I had been promised a government position as a research officer with the Department of Northern Affairs and National Resources, but heard nothing from it. Geoff arranged a six-month contract with the Defence Research Board, which included a return to the Gilman Glacier for three weeks to continue our research there. We left in mid-May 1960, accompanied by Ray Yong, a soil scientist, and landed by ski-wheel DC3 on Lake Hazen on the twentieth of the month. Two days later Geoff and I flew up to our camp on the glacier, finding everything there in good order. The Eliason snow toboggan started without a hitch and we travelled down the glacier and around the ice cap on it, measuring the amount of melt since we left in 1958.

On June 12, 1960, we waited to be picked up after making a landing strip by levelling the ice near our camp. When the plane did not appear, Geoff remarked in his usual confident way, "We might have to walk to Alert." Flight Lieutenant "Shorty" Nicholson, the pilot of the DC3 sent to evacuate us, flew up the wrong glacier before seeing us on the Gilman. He bumped the plane down on our rough landing strip and then prepared for takeoff. That's when trouble began.

The early melt had turned the surface ice slushy and the DC3's skis stuck to it. Turning the plane – no mean feat – Shorty headed back up-glacier and set off again. The aircraft vibrated, swayed and shook and we wondered if we'd take off this time. Shorty fired the JATO bottles at just the right moment and the DC3 wobbled into the air at forty knots, just a touch above its stalling speed. We roared down the Gilman valley, looking down at the river in full spate and a herd of muskoxen running round and round in sheer panic. Geoff and I had left our clothes at the base camp, planning to collect them when we landed there on our way south. The ice near the camp had begun to break up, offering no safe landing place, so Shorty headed for the American base at Thule. Landing there, filthy and unshaven, Geoff and I headed for the Base Exchange, reaching it just before it closed. We had not eaten for fourteen hours, but had to look clean and decent before entering the Officers' Mess. A few hours after leaving the glacier we joined the crew of the DC3 there, clean-shaven and wearing new jackets and shirts. We enjoyed a steak dinner and a stateside show before flying to Ottawa.

At Uplands airport, a staff car awaited us.

The army driver saluted Geoff: "Where do you wish to go, sir?" Geoff thought for a moment, then said, "Wherever you're going."

I was home in an hour.

And so ended my career as an Arctic explorer.

We of Operation Hazen returned to civilization like warriors after a successful foray, weary and exhilarated, changed in indefinable ways. We had not gone to the High Arctic for fame, glory or the desire to conquer new lands, the usual motives for polar exploration. Nor had we gone to test ourselves against nature, another motive for going to extremes. Some of us, including myself, had romantic notions about polar travel. We had not suffered much, though life was never comfortable by southern Canadian standards. Each time I left northern Ellesmere Island, I felt sorrow and elation.

Friends remarked on how lost I seemed in the south. My mind, after months of a life stripped down to its bare essentials, had trouble coping with the complexities of urban life. The world appeared cluttered, and I felt like a time traveller from an antique land unspoiled by humans where nature dominated every aspect of life. Even the miserable summer of 1959 did not change this feeling.

Isolation in the polar regions and elsewhere makes or breaks humans. Raymond Priestley, who served with Shackleton and Scott, wrote in his essay "The Polar Expedition as a Psychological Study" of "the trail of broken men" that such ventures left in their wake. Unable to settle down, forever seeking new challenges in the empty parts of the world to fill the empty places in their lives and hearts, they find no peace in settled lands. In 1921, Shackleton sailed for Antarctica in the *Quest* with no clear plans for his expedition; he died in the following year of a heart attack at forty-eight. Frank Wild, who Shackleton had left in charge of the men of the *Endurance* on Elephant Island, took command of the *Quest* and completed its voyage. Shackleton had summoned him back for his last voyage. On its completion this splendid leader returned to his cotton farm in Africa, which failed. Wild took to drink and died of pneumonia in 1930 at the age of forty-six. Raymond Priestley joined Shackleton's 1907-09 expedition at the age of twenty, without a degree, served with Scott and became a respected academic, dying in 1974 at the age of eighty-eight; he retained his passion for Antarctica, returning there twice in his old age.

In a small way, Operation Hazen unravelled some of the mysteries of an unknown part of Canada. It was a very Canadian expedition, lacking the excessive individualism and over-organization that has marked American ventures while being free of the class-based attitudes so common on British polar sorties. We worked together as equals, sharing our varied skills, knowledge and experiences for the good of the group. For many of us it proved to be the best journey in the world, taking us into a little known part of Canada and undiscovered corners of our own beings.

In the Canadian north I saw the shape of possible futures for Canada and other nations. When caribou fight, they sometimes tangle their horns. Unable to free themselves, the animals struggle until exhausted and slowly die of starvation. Small heaps of bones and the interlocked antlers reveal the futility of this form of mutually assured destruction. The bullet-shattered skulls of muskoxen around Lake Hazen offer mute testimony to their inability to learn how to deal with intruders on their territory. For centuries their defensive stance of forming a circle or a line protected them from wolves, but this confrontational way played into the hands of human hunters who shot down the great animals where they stood. Lichen grow where nothing else will. This symbiotic life form of two elementary plants brings colour to the harshest parts of the world, illustrating the values of complementarity and cooperation.

And so it was with Operation Hazen. We developed symbiotic and mutually beneficial relationships with each other, never seeing ourselves as competitors for fame and glory. In doing so we prepared the way for other scientists to explore and study this beautiful, remote and intriguing part of Canada.

Epilogue: After Hazen

Whom have we conquered? None but ourselves. Have we won a kingdom? No – and yes. We have achieved the ultimate satisfaction, fulfilled a destiny. To struggle and to understand, never this last without the other.

— George Mallory, mountaineer,
lost on Everest in 1924

These words echo the way I felt about my time in the Arctic. In 1960, my life took another direction as I realized I'd reached my level of competence as a glacial meteorologist and moved into the human side of northern development.

Trevor Harwood and Geoff Hattersley-Smith kept scientific research going in northern Ellesmere Island after Operation Hazen. Brian Sagar and John Powell spent the summer of 1959 at the snout of the Gilman Glacier. Our short stay on it in 1960 ensured continuity in the research on its regime. In 1961 Geoff headed an eight-man team, which included Brian and Ian Jackson, that worked at Lake Hazen, on the Gilman and the ice cap and the glaciers draining from it. In the following year the Defence Research Board base moved to the head of Tanquary Fiord. In August 1962, the Canadian Coast Guard Ship *John A. Macdonald* sailed into the ice-free inlet and landed housing, fuel, stores and equipment for the new station; Jim Croal supervised this operation and an airstrip was built here. Research here continued until 1970; the Defence Research Board building now houses the headquarters of the Quttinirpaaq National Park, established in 1988.

In 1971-72, Geoff took leave from the Defence Research Board to write an account of the research in northern Ellesmere Island since his first visit there in 1953. *North of Latitude Eighty* appeared in 1974, the same year that DRB vanished as a separate entity, being absorbed into the Department of National Defence. By then, Geoff had settled in Kent, England. He gave a typically whimsical reason for quitting the Arctic. On his journeys Geoff located cairns and messages left by earlier explorers. In 1972 he landed on a hill behind Fort Conger after spotting a cairn. As he put it: "I hopped out and grabbed a can from the cairn . . . It revealed a note signed G. Hattersely-Smith, 1962. Time to quit this Arctic lark, I thought, which I did in the following year."

Trevor Harwood died in 1984 at the age of sixty-nine. Frank Davies passed away three years earlier, aged seventy-seven; paralyzed during his last illness he set about learning German. Jim Croal lived until 1985, dying at the age of sixty-seven. Roger Deane, our genial companion for two summers, drowned while investigating a wreck at the bottom of Lake Huron; he was fifty-six. Fraser Grant moved out of university life in 1969, started a consulting business and co-authored a standard text on geophysics. Diagnosed with cancer in August 1984, he worked on the second edition of the book until his death at sixty-two in November of that year.

Brian Sagar joined the Geography faculty at Simon Fraser University in 1966 after five years with the Geographical Branch in Ottawa, a federal agency that vanished in the mid-sixties. He died of cancer at the age of sixty-two in January 1990. Brian met his end with courage and grace, believing to the last that life was marvellous. He told his wife Norma to pass on a final message to his friends: "Pip-pip, cheerio!"

Dick Harington organized a Hazen Reunion in Ottawa on May 24, 1999. We missed our two American friends. Terry Moore died of a heart attack in November 1993, at eight-five, Moreau Maxwell of cancer in January 1998 at the age of eighty. Svenn Orvig, who lured me on to Operation Hazen and to whom I'm eternally grateful, died at seventy-eight in 1998. Bob Christie, looking youthful, attended the reunion. He suffered a heart attack at seventy-three while sailing his boat, dying three months later.

The members of the winter party went on to distinguished scientific careers. Outside the Canadian Museum of Nature in Ottawa stand statues of several members of a family of mammoths. A plaque reads: "Dick Harington heard a strange story: A monster had died on the banks of the Yukon's Whitestone River. He decided to explore the river and found a well preserved skeleton of a female woolly mammoth." Dick is one of Canada's leading authorities on ice age vertebrates, arctic and alpine mammals and climatic change in Canada during the ice age. As he puts it: "We scientists are Canadian sovereignty."

After completing his doctorate at McGill, Ian Jackson taught at the London School of Economics before moving to Canada to work on government policy; he served as executive secretary of Sigma XI, the scientific research society, from 1981 to 1987. Dingle Smith, the ever-cheerful lad from Palmers Green, went back to

England in 1959, taught at universities there and emigrated to Australia, retiring from academic life in 1991. John Powell moved to Calgary in 1959 to work for the federal Department of Agriculture, taking up a research post in Edmonton in 1970 dealing with forestry problems. John retired in 1991 and died, aged seventy-two, in August 2005.

Hal Sandstrom studied oceanography in California then settled in Nova Scotia, working for the federal government. Hans Weber joined the Gravity Division of the Dominion Observatory and participated in the Polar Continental Shelf Project for twenty-five years. He retired in 1990 to a three-hundred-acre farm north of Ottawa where he and Meg raise organic cattle.

In organizing the reunion, Dick could not trace John Filo or Barry Walker, nor could he locate Mike. Keith Arnold also served with the Polar Continental Shelf Project and then joined the Glaciology Division of the federal government, retiring in 1986. Unfortunately, I've lost contact with my tent mate. Ian McLaren ended his academic career as a distinguished professor at Dalhousie University in Halifax, retiring in 1996. Jim Soper became Chief Botanist at what was the National Museum of Natural Sciences (now the Canadian Museum of Nature), retiring in 1981. John Tener organized the first aerial wildlife survey of the Queen Elizabeth Islands (the official name of the islands lying beyond 75° N) in 1961 with Dick Harington as one of his assistants. In 1968, he became Director General of the Canadian Wildlife Service, and later Assistant Deputy Minister of Environment Canada. After retiring, John sought new horizons in China, Jamaica, Kenya and Southern Africa and dug up fossils with Dick on Ellesmere Island in 1992-2001.

Merv Utas served with the RCAF in Europe after his sterling work with us. He later provided air support for the UN Military

Observer Mission during one of the disputes between India and Pakistan over Kashmir. This involved landing STOL (Short Take Off and Landing) Caribou aircraft on strips as high as 4,600 metres. Merv left the RCAF in 1970 to join the federal Department of Transport as a civil aviation inspector, retiring in 1987.

The US Coast Guard Cutter *Eastwind*, decommissioned in 1958 and sold to the Gillete company, probably ended up as razor blades, a sad end for such a gallant ship.

Between 1960 and 1966 I worked for the Department of Northern Affairs and National Resources, carrying out studies of squatters, new towns, declining communities, and social and economic change in the Yukon Territory In 1966 I became a professor at Saint Paul University in Ottawa and research director of the Canadian Research Centre for Anthropology. I spent five years teaching and doing research on unemployed youth, northern Scotland, and community development. In 1971 I moved to Antigonish, Nova Scotia, to teach at the Coady International Institute at St. Francis Xavier University. Since 1973 I've lived in Halifax, earning a freelance living as a magazine editor, consultant, writer and association executive and carrying out voluntary assignments in Wales, Scotland, Labrador, Egypt, Lesotho, and with First Nations and Inuit communities.

Northern Ellesmere Island now forms the core of Quttinirpaaq National Park, Canada's second largest. Lake Hazen will again be the site of expeditions during the 2007-08 International Polar Year. Various research projects are planned on the char in the lake and climate change. A Canadian, American and British venture is slated to study the Ward Hunt Ice Shelf.

Northern Ellesmere Island retains its solitary splendour. This remote land can be reached more easily these days, although it is very costly to do so if you go there as a tourist. In our increasingly grim, stressed-out world, a trip to the polar regions is a journey into the heart of lightness, those pure, pristine parts of nature where you plumb the depths of your own being as your spirit soars into the clear blue air. You return to normal life refreshed and renewed as we did on Operation Hazen.

Sources

Atwood, Margaret. *Strange Things. The Malevolent North in Canadian Literature.* Oxford: Clarendon Press, 1995.

Barr, William. *The Expedition of the First International Polar Year 1882-1883.* Calgary: Arctic Institute of North America, 1985.

Barr, William. *Red Serge and Polar Bear Pants: The Biography of Harry Stallworthy, RCMP.* Edmonton: University of Alberta Press, 2004.

Bennett, Jack. *Not Won in a Day: Climbing Canada's Highpoints.* Calgary: Rocky Mountain Books, 1999.

Berton, Pierre. *The Arctic Grail: The Quest for the North West Passage and the North Pole.* Toronto: McClelland & Stewart, 1988.

Cherry-Garrard, Apsley. *The Worst Journey in the World.* London: Constable, 1923.

Dick, Lyle. *Muskox Land: Ellesmere Island in the Age of Contact.* Calgary: University of Calgary Press, 2001.

Fagan, Brian. *The Little Ice Age: How Climate Made History 1300-1850.* New York: Basic Books, 2000.

Gavet-Imbert, Michèle. (Ed.) *The Guinness Book of Explorers and Exploration.* Enfield, Middlesex: Guinness Publishing, 1991.

Greely, Adolphus. *Three Years of Arctic Service.* 2 volumes. New York: Charles Scribner's Sons, 1886.

Guttridge, Leonard F. *Ghosts of Cape Sabine: The Harrowing True Story of the Greely Expedition.* New York: Berkley Books, 2000.

Harington, C.R. (Ed.) *Canada's Hidden Dimension: Science and History in Canada's Arctic Islands.* 2 volumes. Ottawa: Canadian Museum of Nature, 1990.

Harington, C.R. *Operation Hazen (1957-58).* Ottawa: Polar Bear Publishing, 2001.

Hattersley-Smith, Geoffrey. *North of Latitude Eighty: The Defence Research Board in Ellesmere Island.* Ottawa: Information Canada, 1974.

Hattersley-Smith, Geoffrey. *Geographical Names of the Ellesmere Island National Park and Vicinity.* Calgary: Arctic Institute of North America and Parks Canada, 1998.

Jackson, Ian. *Does Anyone Read Lake Hazen?* Edmonton: Canadian Circumpolar Institute, 2002.

Johnson, Clive. The Devil's Labyrinth: Encounters With the Arctic. Swan Hill Press, 1995.

Kobalenko. Jerry. *The Horizontal Everest: Extreme Journeys on Ellesmere Island.* Toronto: Penguin Viking, 2002.

McKinlay, William Laird. *Karluk: The Great Untold Story of Arctic Exploration and Survival.* London: Granada Publishing, 1978.

Moss, John. *Enduring Dreams: An Exploration of Arctic Landscapes.* Toronto: Anansi, 1994.

Perkins, Dennis N.T. *Leading at the Edge: Leadership Lessons from the Extraordinary Saga of Shackleton's Antarctic Expedition.* New York: Amacom, 2000.

Schledermann, Peter. *Voices in Stone: A Personal Journey into the Arctic Past.* Calgary: Arctic Institute of North America, 1996.

Spufford, Francis. *I May Be Some Time: Ice and the English Imagination.* London: Faber and Faber, 1996.

Sboda, Josef and Bill Freedman (Eds). *Ecology of a Polar Oasis: Alexandra Fiord, Ellesmere Island, Canada.* Toronto: Captus University Publications, 1994.

Swan, Robert. *Icewalk.* London: Jonathan Cape, 1990.

Tangye, Nigel. "Introduction," pp. 5-9 in Turner, W.J. (Ed.) *British Adventure.* London: Collins, 1947.

Taylor, Andrew. *Geographical Discovery and Exploration in the Queen Elizabeth Islands.* Ottawa: Queen's Printer, 1955.

Thurston, Harry. "Icebound Eden." *Equinox*, May-June, 1986.

Todd, A.L. *Abandoned: The Story of the Greely Expedition 1881-1884.* New York: McGraw-Hill, 1961.

Victor, Paul-Emile. "Exploration and Adventure" pp. 7-8 in *The Guinness Book of Explorers and Exploration* by Michèle Gavet-Imbert. Enfield, Middlesex: Guinness Publishing, 1991.

Weber, Richard M. et al. *Polar Bridge: An Arctic Odyssey*. Toronto: Key Porter, 1990.

Weber, Richard M. and Mikhail Malakhov. *Polar Attack: From Canada to the North Pole and Back*. Toronto: McClelland & Stewart, 1996.

Werstein, Irving. *Man Against the Elements: Adolphus W. Greely*. New York: Washington Square Press, 1967.

Wheeler, Sara. *Cherry: A Life of Apsley Cherry-Garrard*. New York: Random House, 2002.

Zelder, Martin. "Government Failure at the North Pole." *Fraser Forum*, December 2000.